MODERNITY AND ITS AGENCIES

Modernity and Its Agencies

Young Movements in the History of the South

Edited by

TOURAJ ATABAKI

SEPHIS

MANOHAR
2010

First published 2010

ISBN 978-81-7304-841-8

Published by
Ajay Kumar Jain *for*
Manohar Publishers & Distributors
4753/23 Ansari Road, Daryaganj
New Delhi 110 002

Printed at
Salasar Imaging Systems
Delhi 110 035

Contents

Acknowledgements

The contributions to this volume stem, with a few exceptions, from the workshop on 'Young Movements in the History of the South' which was organized by the South-South Exchange Programme for Research on the History of Development (SEPHIS) at the Uzbekistan Academy of Sciences in Tashkent in autumn 2003.

As part of the organizing team, I greatly appreciate the support I received from Dilorom Agzamovna Alimova (Director of the Institute of History, Uzbekistan Academy of Sciences), Valeriy Sergeevich Khan (Director, International Affairs of the Institute of History, Uzbekistan Academy of Sciences), Willem van Schendel (former Chair, Steering Committee of SEPHIS), Ingrid Goedhart (former Office Manager, SEPHIS) and Jacqueline Rutte (Office Manager, SEPHIS).

In the process of editing this volume, I benefited from the indispensable assistance of Siddharth Chowdhury and Kingshuk Chatterjee who read the manuscript and shared with me their editorial comments. I would like to offer my sincere thanks to them.

Touraj Atabaki

Note on Transliteration

Transliteration is always a thorny problem when one is dealing with several languages at once. There has been no attempt to impose a uniform system of transliteration on the contributions to this volume. Since spellings derived from non-Roman script are often compromises and may always be disputed, and no system is without its anomalies, decision about transliteration have been left to the discretion of individual authors.

CHAPTER 1

Introduction: The Enduring Endeavour of the 'Young': Some Comparative Remarks[1]

Touraj Atabaki

Modernization was a global phenomenon that was launched almost concurrently although with different paces, in different parts of the world. In the political sphere modernization was juxtaposed with the birth of the civil society and the emergence of individualism and individual autonomy, the latter was mainly manifested in the individual's political and civil rights.

Arguably, the age of modernity began with a new era when the basic unit in the structures of a modern society assumed an individualistic character. This approach differed fundamentally from the concept upon which the agrarian or peasant societies were founded. Consequently, class solidarity, ethnic particularism and cultural awareness gave way to a higher degree of social mobilization, and technological and economic integration. At the same time, industrial relations were modernized, articulated and intermingled with individualism and individual autonomy, both of which became an indispensable part of modern man's perception of civility. The idea of individualism that was embodied in the liberty and autonomy of the individual provided a new definition embracing the newly emerged association between the individual and the polity.

Accordingly, the individual in a modern society, at least in principle, was no longer the subject of a priest, a sheikh, a king, a sultan, a shah or a khan endowed with divine or prescriptive authority, but rather was expected to act rationally according to the rule of law. The investiture of new juridical and political rights, including the right of representation, was indeed the ultimate realization of this new association. The emerging commercial and industrial urban middle class was inextricably linked to this individualism.

The political modernity study area is predominantly influenced by the Weberian perception, according to which modernity is assumed as a product of occidental rationality with a general mandate regarding its applicability, irrespective of geography, time, environment, social order or practice. Such perception of modernity, which crafted European historicism, 'posited historical time as a measure of cultural distance (at least in institutional development) that was assumed to exist between the West and non-West (Chakrabarty 2000: 7). Accordingly, non-Western societies were doomed to linger in history's 'waiting-room' to adopt the European model of modernity. Such historicism, as Chakrabarty argues, is 'what made modernity or capitalism look not simply global but rather as something that become global *over time*, by originating in one place (Europe) and then spreading outside it' (Chakrabarty 2000: 7). The 'first-in-Europe-then-elsewhere' structure of global historical time chiefly manifested itself as Eurocentrism and comes into focus when we examine the studies of modernity and the process of modernization in the non-Western societies.

Apart from the issue of Eurocentrism, the study of the practice and institutionalization of political modernity suffers from other deficiencies, namely, assigning the agency to the elite that may include the secular intelligentsia, colonialists and various social or political institutions. By doing so, the historians tend to deny the agency of the non-elite and its autonomous consciousness and dehistoricize the process of social and cultural changes by way of adopting an essentialist approach. It was, indeed, this mode of historiography which gave birth to the school of *subaltern studies* in India in the early 1970s.[2] Although the subaltern historians aimed at criticizing the historiography of Indian nationalism, it has evolved into a critique of historiography itself over the past twenty years. A criterion of such criticism then became its counter-essentialist approach to define the process of social and cultural changes and, hence, deal with the question of identity in writing the past.

In studying the practice of modernity and institutionalization of political modernity, one needs to distinguish between different agencies involved in the process. While the agents of practising modernity in Asia, Europe and Africa were the urban lower and middle classes, the pioneers of institutionalization of political modernity were often a group of young activists with diverse class associations, faith affiliations or political aspirations whose common purpose was challenging the conventional establishment in perusing pervasive change and reform. The 'old' was iconized by the *ancien régime* and its entourages, and the 'young' was idolized by all what was 'not old', often an indistinct insight of what was perceived to be the 'new'. The word 'Young' in both the South and the North soon evolved into the classical epithet of emerging enlightened intelligentsias in their struggles against despotic rule and clericalism. Yet, there were many different meanings that have been attached to the word 'Young' and the political significance of the Young Movement. Neither revivalism, professional elitism, resistance of the Muslim world against Western or Hindu domination, educational aspirations, constitutionalism, authoritarianism, social-democracy, Darwinism, nor radical liberalism can be excluded from the ideological catalogue of the 'Young'. However, with the practice of colonialism and imperial expansionism, the Asian, African or even some European 'Young' often crafted their identity through rejecting and defying the other, i.e. the colonial power. Therefore, the anti-colonial approach of the 'Young' gradually evolved into an inseparable constituent of their bearing upon change and reform.

Yet, there is one question to be answered: should one consider the 'Young' in societies, where modernity is practised, as the pioneers of modernity, 'guiding' the nation to a 'higher stage' of development? The answer to the advocates of the stagiest theory of history, around which European perception of political modernity was centred, is positive. For these historians, the absence of the 'Young' in the introduction and practice of modernity in certain societies is rather a vacant 'waiting room'. However, one could argue that while certain societies had their 'Young', others simply lacked them because there is no 'waiting room' in history.

In this volume, scholars from the South, mainly representing Asia and Africa, have studied merely a selective number of regional and national Young movements. Mansura Haidar, in her article, studies the socio-etymological dimension of the word 'Young' in multi-linguistic spaces. Rosinka Chaudhuri analyses the influence of English literature on the formation of a new identity among the Young Bengal. Nader Devlet's article deals with nineteenth-century Russia and traces the impact of the Tatar Reform Movement upon the wider Turkic world. Samim Akgönül examines the continuity and rapture between the early Young Ottoman and the Young Turks and the widespread changes and reforms practised in the Republic of Turkey by Kemal Atatürk. Diloram Alimova's article explores the ideological dependencies of the reform movements of Central Asia, Persia and the Arab world in the late nineteenth and early twentieth centuries. In the Caucasus, Solmaz Rustamova examines the practice of power in the early years of the Bolshevik regime and, also, the nationalist sentiments practised by a certain segment of the Azeri society. Kaveh Bayat focuses on Iran. In his contribution, Bayat gives more weight to the formation of the Young movement in the Pahlavi era than the reform movement during the nineteenth and early twentieth centuries, which was characterized by the Constitutional Revolution of 1905-9. Finally, Fatima Harrak in her 'Young Modernist *vs.* Old Turbans' studies the triumphs and trials of the reform movement in pre-colonial Morocco.

Undoubtedly, this collection of case studies does not claim to have covered the entire South, nor does it claim to have examined the reform movements in the entirety of the respective regions. By the same token, this introduction does not intend to investigate into the Young movements that have not been independently studied in the volume itself. Nor does it intend to review the collection of case studies presented in this volume. The aim of this introduction is, therefore, twofold: first, to introduce a comparative analysis of the Young movements in Asia and Africa; and second, to highlight the viability of the ideological and inter-organizational dependencies between these movements. Whilst I have not treated the regions under consideration quite evenly, I should add that much needs to be done in order to fully grasp the nature of trans-regional dependencies.

The credit of utilizing for the first time the word 'Young' goes to an Indian reformer of colonial India in the 1820s, when a group of students of Hindu College of Calcutta celebrated a circle of radicals, named as Young Bengal, poised to revolt against the existing social and religious structure of Hindu society.[3] A few years later, in 1838, several members of Young Bengal along with some other former students of Hindu College established the Society for the Acquisition of General Knowledge, devoting themselves to the pursuit of modern knowledge. The Young Bengalis launched their own publications, including numerous periodicals,[4] and attempted to challenge the fundamentals of the then social order. They also contributed to the architecture of an anti-colonial intellectual movement which appeared in the form of the Young Indian a century later and confronted the supremacy of British colonialism.[5]

Following the footsteps of the Young activists in India, an Italian reformist; Giuseppe Mazzini, launched in 1831, his campaign for a united and republican Italy known as the *Giovine Italia* or Young Italy. In 1832, Mazzini published his journal *Giovine Italia* which unfortunately survived for only two years. *Giovine Italia's* claim to the effect that 'all the men of the nation are called by the law of God and Humanity to be free and equal brothers, and only a republic could guarantee this' and his further emphasis on the notion of Italy's unity and creating Italians as a nation, i.e. *Risorgimento*, attracted many Italians to the cause of independence. The rapid increase in the number of people supporting the movement, especially the urban middle class, soon made the *Giovine Italia* as a symbol of modern nation-state building in the nineteenth century. Those who followed Mazzini in Italy, such as Piedmont, or in Germany, Ireland and the Ottoman Empire, were largely affected by Mazzini's egalitarian approach to the individual and its autonomy.

In the early 1830s, the German reformist, Ludolf Wienbarg, in association with his colleagues Karl Gutzkow and Theodor Mundt, launched a social and literary reform movement known as the *Junges Deutschland* or Young Germany. The *Junges Deutschland's* anti-censorship campaign, although launched on a literary platform, was nevertheless, not confined within the literary sphere and added a vocal dimension to Germany's public discourse of civility. Not only did they try to scour the German public consciousness from national romanticism but they also juxtaposed the individual and its autonomy with the authority exercised by the state.

The *Junges Deutschland's* literary campaign was echoed in other parts of Europe with a nationalistic tune. In the early 1840s, a group of Irish intellectuals gathered to reconstruct the Irish identity by advocating the study of Irish history and Gaelic language. Although the crafted Irish nationalism's early target was repealing the 1800 Irish Act of Union with Great Britain, the Young Ireland, through the publication of its weekly journal *Nation*, effectively transformed the early utilitarian and patriotic rhetoric into an integrated linguistic, cultural, historical and non-denominational nationalism. Consequently, for the outside world, specially the colonial world, the Young Ireland movement embodied both the enduring aspiration for independence and the relentless effort to recover a persistently denied past by the colonialists. However, for many pursuing the Young Ireland, the most significant accomplishment of the movement was indeed its ability to secure the support of the Irish intelligentsia, peasantry and urban working-class, which impressed many reformists worldwide.[6]

In the periphery of Europe, the colossal emblem of the 'Young' movement for change and reform was soon centred in the Ottoman Empire.[7] In 1865, in the heart of the old Empire, a group of young intellectuals assembled in Istanbul and formed a society aiming to promote profound reforms within the sultanic regime. The *Ittifak-i Hamiyyet*, Patriotic Alliance, which later came to be known as the Society of Young Ottomans, was originally formed as a political platform aiming to limit the absolute power of the Sultan. The clandestine network of the Young Ottoman soon suffered sustained attacks from the sultanate. However, the core of the group succeeded in escaping to Paris and later to London. While expanding their international contacts, the Young Ottomans began to publish the new inflammatory periodicals of *Hürriyet* (Freedom) and *Mukhbir* (Messenger). Now in exile, they bluntly addressed the Ottoman Sultan that:

> The decadence of the nation and intervention of the Western powers were due to misrule which, in turn, resulted from the absence of liberty. It was not sufficient to make reforms; what was needed was a liberal regime whose continuance was guaranteed. This, though did not mean robbing *Padishah* [Sultan] of his independence, neither did it mean robbing the people of their religion and customs. A liberal regime would ameliorate of the internal maladies, would bring about normal relations with the European powers, and would be equally good for the Muslims because justice was of only one kind. (Berkes 1998: 208)

Furthermore, the Young Ottoman elaborated their call by insisting that in order to observe continuity in sustaining a liberal regime, a 'fundamental law' and a 'national assembly' are needed in the Ottoman Empire. Only through the authority of such an institution, they argued, one could guarantee that the government would be controlled by the people while the monarchy would abide by the rule of law (Berkes 1998: 206).

The need to adopt a civil code of laws for institutionalizing a national government was not a novel idea confined to the Ottoman Empire. In the neighbouring Persian Empire, in 1859, Mirza Malkom Khan (1833-1908) published an excellent treatise: the *Daftar Tanzimat ya Kitabchah Ghaybi* (The Book of Regulations or the Unseen Booklet). In the *Kitabchah Ghaybi*, while he asserted that the government in Iran was 'smitten with plague' and hopelessly backward, he put forward a preliminary draft of a constitution. Some years later in 1870, Yusef Khan Mustashar al-Dawlah published a book on politics, which became the Iranian intellectuals' manifesto against the Shah and his government. In *Risalah Musumah bih Yak Kalamah* (a treatise entitled 'One Word'), Mustashar al-Dawlah stressed the significance of introducing written laws, which should receive the nation's approval in order to define and coordinate its relations with the government (Mustashar ad-Dawlah n.d.: 14). Accordingly, he believed that the origin of state authority stemmed from the nation: 'People's indisputable authority determines the legitimacy of the government performances' (Mustashar ad-Dawlah n.d.: 8).

Likewise, in the Emirate of Bukhara, it was Ahmad Danish who in 1874 persuaded Emir Muzaffar al-Din to implement a series of fundamental reforms in the country (Hadizah 1976: 43). The need for introducing and implementing law in the Emirate was the central theme of Danish's treatise. Those reforms were, however, revealed in a long essay that Danish compiled later in the same year, entitled *Risalah dar Nazm Tamaddun va Ta'avun* (A Treatise on the Order of Civilization and Cooperation) and presented this treatise to Emir Muzaffar al-Din. However, the Emir was willing to implement every conceivable measure to retain his throne other than adopting policies of reform. Danish's proposed reforms were eventually rejected by the Emir.

The reaction of the political establishments in the Persian Empire, the Emirate of Bukhara and the Ottoman Empire towards any call for change and reform was extremely brutal. The fear of the Sultan's reprisal and persecution made many young Ottomans to flee the Empire and find shelter in exile. In Persia, the intelligentsia paid a heavy price for their convictions. In the Qazvin prison, Mustashar al-Dawlah was beaten over his head with his book *Yak Kalamah* so violently that he became blind. In Bukhara Ahmad Danish was forced to withdraw from all government services spending the last twenty-two years of his life as a recluse.

However, if the ideology of loyalty to the state was one which permeated the first generation of the Persian, Ottoman and Central Asian reformists, preventing them from resorting to radical politics, the end of the nineteenth century witnessed the emergence of a new generation of reformists who were prepared to radically challenge the rulers' authority in that region. In Persia, a few years after the assassination of Naser al-Din Shah in 1896, a gargantuan constitutionalist movement accelerated the establishment of the national assembly which warped up the arbitrary rule of the Qajar monarchy in 1906. In the Ottoman Empire, the Young Turks' gunmen seized the Empire's administration in 1908.

For the Persian constitutionalists, the institution of a national assembly was nothing but an essential step towards the foundation of a new Iran. Therefore, to a certain degree, all urban classes participated in a revolution which was 'basically in the long line of historic revolts by the Iranian society against the ancient arbitrary state' (Katouzian 2003: 154). When the Grand National Assembly was inaugurated in August 1906, Sheikh Mahdi, one of the constitutionalists, addressed the crowds thus:

> Today, the Iranians' dark long night of anguish finally came to an end and the sun of fortune and prosperity arose. . . . Now it is for the people who have awaken from lifelong sleep of ignorance to safeguard their essential rights and open a new era to compensate for all of the destruction that the country has suffered. (Kashani 1967: 336)

For many Iranians the Constitutional Revolution was a remedy for the ancient motherland to prevail over her infirmity and reassert her youthfulness when as a young mother she was capable of giving birth to children who, as agents of the land, could preserve her dignity, integrity and sovereignty:

> Having the experience of five thousand years and making two years of strenuous endeavour and sacrificing thousands of innocent souls and sustaining a great deal of time and material loss, we have finally acquired the cure for your feeble and weary spirit and are now providing it to you under the noble call of National Council. Take this remedy and drink it up and feel rejuvenated and continue to nurture your children. (*Sur Israfi*, no. 18, 27 November 1907)

Outside the Iranian Grand National Assembly, while the reformists celebrated the people's will as the foundation of state legitimacy, they did not conceal their anxiety about the old conservative establishment's resumed offensive efforts. In the north-western province of Azerbaijan, the Council of Tabriz followed the political developments in the capital with great concern. When the newly crowned king, Muhammad 'Ali Mirza, began to behave as if he did not recognize the existence of the Grand National Assembly, the Council of Tabriz sent a telegram to the Grand National Assembly presenting seven demands, according to which the Shah would provide authentication to the constitutional government (Kasravi 1977: 214-15). Similarly, when the Shah revealed his opposition to the Grand National Assembly, the Council of Tabriz immediately dispatched a telegram to the provincial councils throughout the country accusing him of 'breaking his promises'. In the same telegram, the Shah was referred to as 'a traitor to the country and to the nation', and a cry was raised again for 'all Iranian brothers to stand up and safeguard the Grand National Assembly and the Constitution' (*Anjoman*, no. 31, 13 June 1908).

Indeed, the Shah broke his promises. He eventually presented the Grand National Assembly with an ultimatum and three days later, on 23 June 1908, he ordered the bombardment of the premises of the Grand National Assembly and thus began a new chapter in the Iranian Constitutional Revolution (Malekzadeh 1984: 706, 748-60; Kasravi 1977: 631-57). The thirteen months from June 1908 to July 1909 which followed the king's *coup d'état* were a decisive stage in the constitutional movement in Iran. Despite the fact that, for the time being at least, the *coup* successfully hindered the functioning of a constitutional government, the overall long-term effect of the Shah's violent intervention helped to further galvanize the movement. The propertied classes, who rather easily abandoned the barricades in the early days of the movement and, in some cases, even pretended that social harmony prevailed throughout the nation, were now shocked into a new consciousness. It was quite obvious that the constitutional movement had the capacity to bring about profound changes to the traditional sociopolitical structures. On the other hand, the subaltern was coming to realize that a constitutional government did not result in everyone 'eating a kebab as long as the span of a hand'. The latter quotation refers to a statement made by one of the proponents of the revolution, Sheikh Salim. During the early days of the movement in Tabriz, he had assured the people that when the constitution came into being, such would be the benefits which they would enjoy (Kasravi 1977: 216). According to an eyewitness account:

> In Tabriz during the Constitutional Revolution as in Paris during the French Revolution, the *sans-culottes* and the poor reared their heads. The driving

force of these men was towards anarchy. First to overthrow the despotic power of the Court, then to turn against the rich and propertied classes. It was with the backing of such men that Danton and Robespierre rose to power. In Tabriz no Danton and Robespierre appeared but if they had, we would have had our own *reign of terror*. Instead we lived through a period of chaos, instability and fear. (Kasravi 1977: 355)

Following thirteen months of bloody civil war, the coordinated efforts of the Iranian constitutionalists succeeded in deposing the Shah. The constitutionalist armed forces, who had formulated a series of demands, were closing in on the capital from north and south. By now it was too late for the king to redeem the situation by accepting the demands of the constitutionalists. The Shah was finally forced to abdicate. In the summer of 1909, the political scenario in Iran differed significantly from what it was four years earlier. The dramatic events of the civil war served to accelerate the rise of political awareness, especially class consciousness and ethnic identity. The outcome of the Iranian constitutional crisis was nothing but the exclusion, albeit temporarily, of the *old reactionaries* from the country's executive institutions by the *young revolutionaries.*

In the midst of the Iranian constitutional crisis, in the neighbouring Ottoman Empire, a new Young movement, now called the Young Turks led a revolutionary movement against the authoritarian regime of Sultan Abdülhamid II. The Young Turks was a coalition of various reformist groups, aimed at establishing a constitutional government in an Empire which was facing a dramatic decline in all fronts. The organization of the Young Turks dates back to 1889 when a group of students of the Imperial Military Medical College of Istanbul formed the Ottoman Unity Society. Over the next few years, the society's most activists were either arrested by the Ottoman police or were sent into exile, mainly into Paris. At the early stage, the activities of these political émigrés were confined to publishing pamphlets and periodicals. However, there were some individuals amongst these constitutionalist émigrés who opted for more disciplined political actions aiming at introducing orderly reform under a functional central government and the exclusion of European influence. The most notable figure among these individuals was Ahmet Riza who became the spokesperson of the newly founded organization known as the Committee of Union and Progress (CUP). In the following years what was left from the Ottoman Unity Society joined CUP and adopted its name. The group called itself *Jeunes Turc* and published a bilingual periodical *Meşveret* (Consultation)[8] in which they openly challenged the authoritarian rule of Abdülhamid II.

Following the aborted *coup d'état* of 1896, which ended with the mass arrest of CUP activists, the leadership of the committee suffered from political factionalism and fragmentation. However, in 1906 and with the emergence of the Ottoman Freedom Society in Salonika (today Thessaloníka, Greece) and its final merger with the CUP, the Young Turks were now poised to seize power in Istanbul. The defeat of the old foe, the Russian Empire, in the Russo-Japanese War of 1905, followed by revolutions in Russia and neighbouring Iran, left their mark on the Young Turks' collective destiny. A definite drive behind the final assault was when the dissident member of the Third Army Corps in Macedonia, one of the founders of the Ottoman Freedom Society, marched towards Istanbul and called for the restoration of the Ottoman Constitution which had been prorogued since 1878. They then, put an end to the thirty years' authoritarian rule of Sultan Abdülhamid II and forced him to the power yield in July 1908.

The trans-national solidarity between the Youngs did not confine itself to the ideological framework, yet it often found its way into the practical realm. For example, while the Iranian constitutional revolution of 1906 inspired the Young Turks to attain political power in 1908, it was the Young Turks who in a reciprocal comradely act extended their solidarity to the Persian revolutionaries following the Persian king's *coup d'état* in June 1908. In November 1908, a delegation of leading figures of the Ottoman CUP visited the Iranian constitutionalist in Tabriz. By this time, the Unionists were in power in Istanbul and their pro-Iranian constitutionalist policy could indeed jeopardize their relation with Teheran. Nevertheless, in their visit to Tabriz, while the CUP men awarded Sattar Khan, a renowned Iranian constitutionalist leader, with an Ottoman CUP medallion, they offered their sympathy and support to the Iranian constitutionalists (*Nalih Millat*, no. 27, 20 November 1908). The newspaper *Nalih Millat* (People's Cry), published in Tabriz, while reporting the news, marked the event as 'a sign of unity amongst all freedom lovers in the region'.

On the other side of the Caspian Sea, the news of the Persian and Turkish constitutionalists encouraged a new generation of reformists in Central Asia. As has been discussed in details in both Nadir Devlet's and Dilaram Alimova's articles later in this volume, the reform movement in Central Asia for a long time had been inspired by the Tatar, Ottoman, Persian, Arab and Indian reform movements of the late nineteenth–early twentieth centuries. While Ahmad Danish represented an era of Russian supremacy in the region, by the end of the nineteenth century and with the expansion of Russian colonial rule in the Caucasus and Central Asia, the new generation of the Central Asian reformists, who soon became known as the *Jadidists*,[9] engaged vehemently in challenging both the traditional establishment and the colonial rule of imperial Russia.

The early contact between the reformist individuals in Bukhara and their fellow-thinkers on the other side of the Caspian Sea, namely, in the Caucasus and Iran, dates back to the last decade of the nineteenth century. According to a report by a British agent in the region,[10] in the late nineteenth century, the newspaper *Akhtar* (Star) was widely circulated in Central Asia. *Akhtar* was one of the early prominent reformist Persian periodicals which had been issued outside Iran. Edited by Muhammad Tahir Tabrizi, *Akhtar* was first published in Istanbul in 1875 and survived quite extraordinarily until 1894. The radical reformist partiality of *Akhtar*, soon made it one of the most influential voices for promoting social justice in the Persian-speaking region.

Another influential Persian periodical distributed in Central Asia was *Qanun* (Law). According to an account published in the Russian periodical *Turkistanskie Vedomosti* in 1898, *Qanun* had a wide circulation in Turkistan (*Turkistanskie Vedomosti*, no. 48, 1898). Edited by the dissident Iranian statesman, Mirza Malkum Khan Nazim al-Dawlah, the first issue of *Qanun* was published in 1890 in London and within fifteen years of its existence became one of the most popular anti-establishment reformist periodicals in the Persian language. Among the various subjects that Malkum Khan treated in *Qanun* were topics such as protest against the condition of lawlessness (*Qanun*, no. 17, no date), the need for a grand national assembly (*Qanun*, no. 6, July 1890), and even his strong belief in the application of Islamic jurisprudence in any future *just society* (*Qanun*, no. 21, no date). *Qanun's* call for change and reform soon found its way to Central Asia. Of the various routes available for *Qanun* to reach Bukhara, such as the one via Baku and Krasnovodsk, one may single out the passage from Calcutta via Kabul and Termez to Bukhara. Since the sixteenth century, Persians had formed one of the most prosperous and learned communities in India.

The third Persian periodical which was also widely welcomed in the intellectual circles in Turkistan in the late nineteenth and early twentieth centuries was *Habl al-Matin* (Firm Cord), whose editor was Sayyad Jalal al-Din Mu'ayid al-Islam Kashani (d'Encausse 1988: 102). Following his meeting with Malkum Khan and on the latter's advice, Kashani launched the publication *Habl al-Matin* in 1892 in Calcutta. In addition to news and analysis of the Iranian political situation, this periodical also paid great attention to the Russian policies in the occupied Caucasus and Central Asia. Issues concerning everyday life in the Emirate of Bukhara were also an important topic that *Habl al-Matin* often tackled in its editorials. *Habl al-Matin's* critical stance on Russian policies in the Caucasus and Central Asia eventually led to its total ban in the Empire's sphere of influence.[11]

In addition to these periodicals, which were affiliated to the Iranian reformist circles, there was another Persian journal in circulation in Central Asia, the *Siraj al-Akhbar* (News Light), published by Mahmud Tarzi in 1911 in Kabul.[12] As an anti-colonialist newspaper with a startling slogan of 'Asia for Asians', *Siraj al-Akhbar's* circulation soon expanded to the north and within two years it claimed to have some 50-60 subscribers in the cities of Bukhara and Samarqand (*Siraj al-Akhbar*, no. 2, 1913). Apparently, the favourable reception of *Siraj al-Akhbar* amongst the Central Asian intellectual circles made Russian authorities outlaw the circulation of this newspaper both in Turkistan and the Emirate of Bukhara (*Siraj al-Akhbar*, no. 2, 1913). However, according to some accounts, the secret circulation of *Siraj al-Akhbar* in the region continued until its closure in 1919 (Habibi 1993: 97).

The Jadidists originally followed the Tatar's perceptions of change by means of introducing modern education to the younger generation. Following the footsteps of Ismail Gasprinski, the Crimean Tatar reformist, who in 1884 founded a new school known as *Usul-i Savtiya* or *Usul-i Jadid* (New Method) school,[13] the Central Asian reformists (*Jadidists*) launched their politico-literary campaigns. They embarked upon founding modern schools and published numerous primers as well as general information books which continued over the first two decades of the twentieth century. Their publishing activities were further boosted by the introduction of Central Asian vernacular newspapers and magazines in 1912. *Bukhara Sharif* (Noble Bukhara), a Persian-language newspaper was founded in Bukhara in March 1912. Its editor, Mirza Jalal Yusufzadeh who was of an Azerbaijani origin, was brought in from Baku. Before departing for Bukhara, Yusufzadeh, a veteran journalist, was the editor of *Haqiqat* (Truth), a weekly magazine published from Baku. *Haqiqat* covered issues ranging from literature, culture and society to politics and economics, that mainly affected the Turkic–Muslim world. In *Bukhara Sharif*, Yusufzadeh successfully endeavoured to produce almost the same quality as *Haqiqat*, covering detailed regional and world news. Further, he called upon the local intellectuals to join his campaign of 'disseminating information and knowledge amongst people' through the *Bukhara Sharif's* pages:

> Up until now, there has existed no newspaper in national and Islamic language in the Emirate of Bukhara with its three million inhabitants or in Turkistan and Transoxiana with their nine to ten million-strong population. . . . With the assistance of some honourable free-thinking Bukharaians [Mirza Mohi al-Din Mansour, Mirza Sarraj Hakim, Haidar Khawjeh Mirbadal, Sadr al-Din 'Ayni and 'Abdulraouf Fitrat], *Bukara-ye Sharif*, as the first Persian newspaper published in the national language of Bukhara, has endeavoured to raise Bukharains' awareness and contribute to

the development and prosperity of our ancestral homeland. (*Bukhara Sharif*, no. 15, 1912)

During the ten-month period of its publication, the *Bukhara Sharif* often tackled issues such as individual and social liberty, and the need for change and reform in Central Asia.

One of *Bukhara Sharif's* main concerns was the launch of an educational campaign to combat illiteracy in the region. It also claimed that this could only be achieved through establishing modern schools and initiating reforms in the curricula. *Bukhara Sharif* did not hesitate to make a reference to the need for educational reforms in almost every single issue. Although the editor was extremely careful not to jeopardize its already vulnerable relation with the Russian authorities, the Emir and the local clerics, its existence as a source of awareness could by no means be tolerated by the pro-Russian establishment. Finally, after distributing 153 issues, at the instigation of the Russian political agent in Bukhara, the Emir banned the publication of *Bukhara Sharif* in January 1913.

These brief comparative remarks about the Young movements in Asia would not be complete if no reference is made to Africa. In her contribution to this volume, Fatima Harrak has adequately dealt with the reform movement in Maghrib. Almost at the same time, in Tunisia, with the establishment of the French protectorate which was introduced in 1883, the political tensions were running high. In 1907, young Tunisians founded a political party and openly expressed their resentment of the establishment.[14] The party which was known in French as *Les Jeunes Tunisiens* (Young Tunisians) called for the country's sovereignty through the total control of the government by Tunisians as well as the recognition of equal rights for the entire nation; the Tunisians and the French alike.

The Young Tunisian party's anti-colonial stance became even more radical when the French administration claimed as public property, the Muslim cemetery. An all-out labour strike and mass demonstrations which ended with boycotts, riots and bloody confrontations turned the Young Tunisians from a small middle-class elite party into the vanguard of the anti-colonial struggle. In 1912, the French responded by making mass arrests and imprisoning the Young Tunisian activists and, furthermore, driving them underground or into exile.

The youth movements in India, Tunisia, Iran, Turkey, Europe and Central Asia have made their voices heard creating demand for change and reform for nearly two centuries. Some of these movements have emerged almost simultaneously regardless of the nature and type of colonialism and despotism in Asia and Africa. Evidently, the word 'Young' has travelled widely and has become an organizational label in, e.g. Turkey, Persia, Bukhara, Tunisia, Myanmar, Java, Senegal, and Nigeria, influencing many Arab countries and Muslim intellectuals in South Asia, Malaysia and Indonesia in their pursuit of liberty and equality.

To avoid essentialism, one should also reflect on the metamorphosis that some young movements adapted throughout the world. In some countries, there were offshoots of the main flow of the young movements that through the resumption of political power joined the old stream of the establishment and lost their initial popular appeal and legitimacy. In other countries, they maintained an authoritarian role in pursuing modernization whilst denying the agency of the subaltern in shaping the polity. In such cases, these movements caused social alienation and gradually developed into isolated elite cliques creating dramatic social raptures. Arguably, the young's innovative call for change and reform, their initiation in ending arbitrary rules, their effort in strengthening the rule of law, and above all their successes and failures can be the subject of further studies. It seems that the young still have a long way to go.

NOTES

1. I would like to extend my gratitude to Reza Jafari for his comments while preparing this Introduction.
2. For a history of subaltern studies, see Prakash 1994: 1475-90.
3. There are numerous studies on Bengal in the nineteenth century and on the origin, time and the records of Young Bengal. See for example Chattopadhyay (1965), Chatterjee (1993).

4. See Mansura Haidar's chapter in the present volume.
5. In 1919, an English weekly *Young India* was published from Calcutta. Edited by Mahatma Gandhi *Young India* continued its publication for twelve years (1919-31). *Young India* was indeed a symbol of struggle against the British colonial rule and it advocated social reform in India.
6. For a comprehensive study of Young Ireland movement see Davis (1987).
7. For a comprehensive study of Young Ottoman see Mardin (1962).
8. For a detailed study of the formation of the Committee of Union and Progress and its early activities see Hanioğlu (2001).
9. For further study of the Jadidists, see Khalid (1998).
10. Colonel Yate to Foreign Office, 8 August 1894. Cited in Parvin (1998).
11. Georgian State Archive, Tbilisi. File 5259, fond, no. 13. Telegram of Russian Ministry of Foreign Affairs to the Governor General of the Caucasus, 22 April 1913.
12. http://links.jstor.org/sici?sici=0305-6139%281980%297%3A2%3C118%3ATANSA%3E2.0.CO%3B2-H&size=LARGE
13. See Nadir Devlet's essay in the present volume.
14. For the study of Young Tunisians, see Ziadeh (1962).

REFERENCES

Berkes, Niyazi, *The Development of Secularism in Turkey*, 2nd edn. (London: Hurst and Company, 1998).

Chakrabarty, Dipesh, *Provincializing Europe: Postcolonial Thought and Historical Difference* (Princeton: Princeton University Press, 2000).

Chatterjee, Partha, *The Nation and its Fragments: Colonial and Postcolonial Histories* (Princeton: Princeton University Press, 1993).

Chattopadhyay, G., *Awakening in Bengal in Early Nineteenth Century* (Calcutta: Progressive Publishers, 1965).

Davis, Richard, *The Young Ireland Movement* (Dublin: Gill and Macmillan, 1987).

d'Encausse, Hélène Carrère, *Islam and the Russian Empire, Reform and Revolution in Central Asia* (London: Tauris, 1988).

Habibi, Abdulhay, *Jonbesh Mashrutiyat dar Afghanistan* (Kabul: n.p., 1993).

Hadizah, Rasul, *Ahmad Danish* (Dushanbeh: 'Irfan, 1976).

Hanioğlu, Sükrü, *Preparation for a Revolution: The Young Turks 1902-1908* (London: Oxford University Press, 2001).

Kashani, Nazim al-Islam, *Tarikh Bidari Iraninan* (Tehran: Bunyad Farhang Iran, 1967).

Kasravi, Ahmad, *Tarikh-e Mashruteh-e Iran* (Tehran: Amir Kabir, 1977).

Katouzian, Homa, *Iranian History and Politics: The Dialectic of State and Society* (London and New York: Routledge Curzon, 2003).

Khalid, Adeeb, *The Politics of Muslim Cultural Reform: Jadidism in Central Asia* (Berkeley, University of California Press, 1998).

Malekzadeh, M., *Tarikh-e Enqelab-e Mashrutiyat-e Iran*, vol. 4, 2nd edn. (Tehran, 'Elmi, 1984).

Mardin, Şerif, *The Genesis of Young Ottoman Thought* (Princeton: Princeton University Press, 1962).

Mustashar ad-Dawlah and Yusif Khan, *Risalah Musumah beh Yak Kalemaeh* (Paris: n.p., undated).

Parvin, Nasealdin *Tarikh-e Rouznamehnegari-ye Iranian va degar Parsi-Nevisan*, vol. 1 (Tehran: Nashr Danishgahi, 1998).

Prakash, Gyan, 'Subaltern Studies as Postcolonial Criticism', *American Historical Review*, vol. 99, no. 5 (1994).

Ziadeh, Nicola A., *Origins of Nationalism in Tunisia* (Beirut: American University of Beirut, 1962).

CHAPTER 2

The Origin, Genesis and Regional Chain Reaction of the 'Young' Movement

MANSURA HAIDAR

In world history, there are very few movements which have had such a widespread chain reaction, identical social and political reasons and repercussions, similar origin, trends and developments simultaneously engulfing at least half of the globe with the same nomenclature, as the 'Young' movement. In this paper, an attempt is being made to discuss various aspects of this humanistic and all-pervading movement.

The first part highlights the literary, etymological, allegorical and figurative significance of the word 'Young' in various oriental languages and their usages in different contexts. The second part deals at length with the genesis and reasons of the application of this word 'Young' to various movements. The third part gives a short summary of various Young or new movements in Central, West and South Asia; and the fourth provides an insight into the nature and complexion of different Young movements and their impact on each other and mutual exchanges in the origin, extent and trends of these movements, with an account of the indigenous shape they took and the influence they wielded on the freedom fighters struggling against various forces.

The itinerary of the word 'Young' offers interesting material for etymological study. In most oriental languages, such as Arabic, Persian, Turkish, Uzbek, Pashto, etc., the term 'Young' is interestingly synonymous with the term 'new' or is used as a qualifying prefix to indicate Young. For example, the words in these languages which stand for the above-mentioned meaning are *nav*, *nau*, *jadid naya*, *navin*, *yeni* or *yangi*. In Persian, the word *nav* means 'a hero, brave man, courageous, weeping, motion, action, trembling; name of a note in music' whereas a similar word *nau, nav, nau, no* stands for 'new; fresh'. The prefix *nau* is applied to a newborn (*nau zaida* or *nau zad*), *nau roz* (new year's day), *nau khez* or *nau khast* for newly arisen. *Nauroziay* (new year's gift); *nau-damida* (newly sprung up, a fresh shoot); *nau daulat* (parvenu, an upstart). The word *nau-jawan* similarly denotes 'young man, lad, youth'; the word *naujawani* refers to 'youth and prime of life' and *nau abadi* to new settlement. Similarly, in Hindi, the word *nav* is used as a prefix *nav yug* (new age), *nav yuvak* (lad, young boy). A new village in Khurasan was named *nauzad*. In Turkish and Uzbek languages, there are two words *jadid* and *yangi,* both of which mean 'new,' the latter, however, also signifies 'young'. In Arabic, the word *jadid* stands for 'new, modern, fresh, new cloth recently cut from the loom, death, the surface of ground, a river in *yamamah*'. The word *yangi* means new in Turkish and the word *cherik* denotes army—the two words *yeni-cheri* or *yangi-cherik* together means 'new forces'. It is surmised that when the Ottomans wanted to create a new and competent cadre of soldiers through a mechanism of converting from Christianity to Islam they called it *yangi cherik* (new force) or *yanicheri* (another new force). It was later on corrupted through consistent use as *janissari*. This band of soldiers proved to be the prop and pillar of the Ottoman strength. The newly established towns or newly renovated and recently spruced up cities often had the prefix *yingi* attached to their proper names as in the case of Autrar, Taraz, Hisar in Central Asia or New attached to the cities of Delhi, York, Jersey, and so on. The new roads or passes also had this word *yingi* or *yangi* clubbed to them, e.g., *yangi-yul* (new road, new pass) which stood next to Parwan and passed through Watian to Khinjan or *yang bulagh* (new spring), which was a road to Kabul.

A number of places elsewhere also carry the prefix 'new', probably because the area thus named 'new' was comparatively a more modern and improved version of the old city, more spruced up and majestic. Besides, the word 'yung' in Chinese means 'brave', and the word was attached to the names of famous elites such as Yung Cheng, Yung-Lo, Yung Wing, Yang His Min (*Dictionary:*

421-2; Isaac 1969: 123, 143, 177, 216, 279; Samson: 1963: 115, 233).

A careful study of the word 'young' in oriental languages proves that it was not only used in the context of anything new as mentioned above, e.g. cities, army detachments, palaces, newspapers, but also the term was particularly and enthusiastically applied to highlight the distinctive characteristics or to exhibit the 'extraordinary' importance of anything which was actually different and remarkable (or gave the semblance of being rare or peculiar or was presented or treated as a unique feature due to some political or personal reasons. The 'classical epithet' of new or young was, therefore an idiom of distinction or a signal heralding of a novel reform experience. It was used for many such political movements which arose out of a watershed in a stage of metamorphosis of the country's religio-political or socio-economic transformation.

In the nineteenth and twentieth centuries, therefore, several movements sprang up throughout Eurasia which had the word 'young' attached to them. Apart from the 'Young Bengal movement' in India, there were several other movements in many parts of the globe where 'Young' or 'new' movements led by enlightened people and ideas brought reforms.

It should be noted here that these 'Young movements' were neither the result of sudden outbursts of an emotional or reactionary nature nor were these rootless phenomena without target or objectives. The very fact that they sprouted and grew almost simultaneously in every corner of Asia proves beyond doubt that they had very solid and valid reasons for outgrowth. Throughout the nineteenth century, there were struggles of Asians against the colonialists in an isolated manner. Towards the end of the nineteenth century another wave of such uprisings engulfed the Asian lands.[1] From the first decade of the twentieth century the third spurt of revolts started.[2] Sometimes and in certain regions, there were the forces of regionalism, Asianism, pan-Turkism, pan-Islamism or any other kind of pan-ism which seem to have played a vital role in bringing the youth together as they were comparatively more sensitive to the surroundings. The predicament and helplessness of subjugation in which the Asians were placed due to the all-pervading imperialist onslaught created simultaneously a feeling of remorse over their pathetic plight and a desire to get out of slumber and strive to make the best out of a bad bargain. Whether it was the defeat of Russia by Japan in 1905, or overthrow of the Qing dynasty by Sun Yat Sen, even a small flicker of victory kindled in them the flames of hope of Asian triumph over unwanted and expanding influence of Imperialist countries. These Young leaders proved to be tutors of a whole new sprouting and upcoming generations.

Thus the word 'New' or 'Young' was attached to many movements which sprang up in Asia during the nineteenth and twentieth centuries. Either these were movements led by the young and supported by the youth or merely the term 'New' or 'Young' was prefixed to it because the youth symbolized zest, enthusiasm, energy, newness and beginning of a new era.

The forms and norms of every region had their own peculiar shades and shadows in this regard but generally the goal was one and the same, i.e. modernization, reform, progress and ascension. This was a wave which engulfed the region extending from the farthest corner of Mongolia, Central Asia, Iran, Turkey, India, Japan, Vietnam, Burma, Indonesia, Malaysia and other places.

Sometimes the influence of pan-Islamism and pan-Turkism had set the scene, at other times the repercussions of Caliphate movement—the sympathy wave towards Turkey due to harsh treatment meted out by Western allies to the Ottomans ignited the Asian emotions. The Russian conquests of Central Asia following the Great Game and Russian Revolution of 1905 had transformed the political scenario.

Imbued with the spirit of idealism, inspired by the ideas of liberty, fraternity, liberalism, *hurriyat*, *watan*, ignited by the fury of surrounding corruption and need for reforms, emboldened by the revolutionary zeal of the age, the youth of this age plunged into reformist activities. The abundant courage, ceaseless vigour, and reckless zest of youth heightened these ambitions to create a Utopia—a world of his own dreams and making. Collective strength further sharpened the edges of their claws to strangle any and every force which hampered their union, active progress and efforts. In an age of transition when most of the Asian countries in their keenness to look ahead were looking back, coddling between the forces of conservatism and progressivism, these 'Young movements' occurred like a chain event in the process of metamorphosis bringing in their wake a spurt of revivalism, reformist activities, revolutionary movements and acquisition of their ultimate goal.

A number of protests or revolutionary movements all over the world had the word 'Young' prefixed to them. When the Irish nationalist organization was established in 1840 by William Smith O'Brien (1803-64), it was named as 'Young Ireland'. O'Brien had led a peasant movement against the British in Tipperary (1848). He was to be put to death on charges of treason but was finally pardoned. Charles Edward Stuart who extended his claims to the Scottish and English thrones was called the 'Young Pretender' (*Dictionary*: 639).

In *Akyuz Antoloji*, Sadullah Pasha's (1838-91) ode to the nineteenth century best summarizes the situation which facilitated the upsurge of 'Young movements' in the Asian region:

The rights of persons and possessions are protected from—attack,
A new order has been given to the world of civilization,
Amr is not Zeyd's slave nor is Zeyd Amr's master,
A clear and indubitable rule establishes the basis for equality.
The spread of science has enlightened the minds of men,
The printing press has completed what was lacking,
Alas the western lands have become the daysprings of knowledge,
Nothing remains of the fame of Rum and Arab, of Egypt and Herat,
The time is a time of progress, the world is a world of science,
Is the survival of societies compatible with ignorance? (Lewis 1968: 133-4)

The poem brings to the fore the undercurrents of Asian people's ambitions, aspirations, marked by a sense of negation, self and survival. The struggle for ascension and for compensating the losses they had suffered due to their comparative backwardness and ignorance, its soaring realization combined with self-assertion goaded them to move step by step to their destination through various methods which suited best to their land and its peoples. It has generally been assumed that in this task they had emulated the examples of the West following the same path and adopting, by and large, the similar methods. Most of the Young movements in Asia had drawn their inspiration from the 'Young Ottoman' and 'Young Turk' movements. The origin of this name 'Young Turks' is said to have emanated from '*Jeune Turquie*'. It is recorded that

> at the beginning of February 1867 the Belgian newspaper *Le Nord* had published [a] report that prince Mustafa Fazil had founded a banking establishment in Turkey. In a letter correcting this mis-statement, the prince referred to his supporters in Turkey as '*Jeune Turquie*' a phrase that was no doubt inspired by the Young Italy, Young France, Young Germany of earlier decades in Europe. This dimenti was copied from the Belgian paper by *Courrier d'Orient* of Pera, the editor of which was on friendly terms with the Ottoman liberals, and thence translated into Turkish in the *Mukhbir* of 21 February 1867. The name appealed to Ali Suavi and Namik Kemal, who tried various Turkish equivalents for it, eventually deciding on Yeni Osmanliler—New or Young Ottomans. This together with the French *Jeune Turcs* appeared as the heading of the publications of the groups. (Lewis 1968: 153-4)

These comments of Bernard Lewis amply testify to the origin of the term and that of the movement which purportedly had its roots in Europe: Elsewhere he had again pointed out that:

> ... in the Europe of the mid nineteenth century, there was no lack of ideologies of revolt. Islam was no longer insulated. Young France, Young England, Young Germany, were an inspiration to Young Turkey also. Turkish students and diplomats witness—may even have shared in—the heart lifting events of 1848. After the suppression of the Hungarian rising of that year, a number of Hungarian and also some Polish revolutionaries sought refuge in Turkey. As rebels against Russia and Austria, they could be sure of a sympathetic welcome and this time they brought new ideas against which their hosts were no longer immune. (Lewis 1968: 135)

Another proof of inspiration from Western influence was that the first organized opposition group was established in 1889 on the first centenary of the French Revolution. The movement thereafter gathered momentum under Prince Sabaheddin (1877-1948). The realization that a revolution cannot be made successful merely by propaganda and publication, led to an unsuccessful military coup followed by the formation of numerous revolutionary societies (Lewis 1968: 196).

In Paris, Prince Sabahuddin initiated 'the League for Private Initiative and Decentralization' and its name was again taken from the French Writer Edmond Demolins' book *A quoi tient la Supériorité des Anglo-Saxons* (1897). This book was translated into different languages and Demolin's thesis that 'superiority of the Anglo Saxons rested on their superior education which developed personality and individual initiative—confidence in oneself, instead of confidence in collectivity usual in other human societies' seems to have had a greater impact on the Arabs and Turks alike and particularly on Sabahuddin whose idea of a federalized and decentralized state was drawn from Demolin's conceptual formulations. Gradually the centre for gravity shifted from the lands beyond Turkey to the homeland and from hands of the exiled to that of the indigenous people. In Turkey a new revolutionary group started actively pursuing their objective in Macedonia and Anatolia. In September 1907, the merger of external and internal strength represented by two groups, namely, Salonica and the Committee of Union and Progress Organization of Paris, rejuvenated and invigorated the movement (Lewis 1968: 202-6).

The Young Turks movement appears to be a replica of the Young Ottoman movement of 1860-70. While the Young Ottomans were confident of saving the Empire, the Young Turks shunned from it. The literary renaissance and the periodical press were not the only contribution of the Young Ottomans, who wanted to

> reconcile the new institutions of the Tanzimat with the Ottoman and Islamic political traditions. The Young Ottomans sought the best of both the worlds; they called for revitalization of the Empire through the incorporation of selected European models and at the same time insisted on the retention of the Islamic foundations of state and society. Theirs was the complex vision of reformers and preservers. (Ahmad 1969: 15-18, 23, 156-7, 161-5; Cleveland 1984: 124-6, 132, 169)

For reawakening, the publication, press and propaganda seemed to be easier methods. From London, Ali Suavi, one of the Ottoman Turks, started the publication of *Mukhbir* (from 31 August 1867). A year later, in 1868, the Young Ottomans published their newspaper *Hurriyet* when *Mukhbir* was closed following Ali

Suavi's re-location to Paris, a new journal called *Ulum* was started by him. Since the Young Ottomans had two main principles, i.e. patriotism (emanating from the precept 'Love of one's country is part of Faith') and the plea for consultative and representative government—(based on the precept 'consult with them in the matter'). The concept of equality enshrined in the Sharia and confirmed through the decrees of 1839 and 1856. In 1860-70 Namik Kemal had again stressed patriotism through his play *Watan*. The Young Turk movement comprised three different protest groups—'one, the exiled community of long-standing; the second, a collection of discontented civil servants and students, and the third a coalition of disaffected army officers stationed in the Ottoman Empire' (Cleveland 1984: 126, 130-1). The constitutional changes of 1908 and the abdication of Sultan Abdul Hamid II (1909) owe their occurrence to this movement which strengthened during the Balkan wars (1912-13) and facilitated Turkish linkages with the German Empire. The leaders of the Committee of Union and Progress, 'committed to the concept of Ottomanism' for over half a century found their policies being contradicted by the occurrence of events during 1908-13. The First World War had, without much hassles, 'cast out' the 'existing monarchies' (Cleveland 1984: 23, 164).

The Turkish literary review *Young Pens* (*Genc Kalemler*) was founded in 1911 and Zia Gökalp (1876-1924), the outstanding theoretician of the Turkish movement became its regular contributor. Gradually, the Young Turk movement spread over a larger area taking the form of pan-Turkism and pan-Islamism. In one of Zia Gökalp's poems 'Turan' published in 1911, the affinity of the Ottoman Turks with the Turanian Turks and the feeling of 'pan-Turanianism' and pan-Turkism is too apparent to be missed:

The country of the Turks is not Turkey, nor yet Turkistan;
Their country is a vast and elernal land: Turan.

The dream of unification of all the Turkic-speaking peoples of Turkey, Persia, Russia, Afghanistan and China under one banner was to be achieved through a 'political programme' in which the exiles and immigrants from the Russian Empire were also to play a significant role and Russia could be outmanoeuvred with the assistance of the Western States. When World War in 1914 found Turkey and Russia arrayed against each other, Zia Gökalp like others of his hopeful allies, once again emphasized in his poem Kizil Destan (Red epic):

The land of the enemy shall be devastated
Turkey shall be enlarged and become Turan. (Lewis 1968: 351)

The Ottoman Turks perhaps also valued this bond of consanguity and kindred relationship with the same intensity and 'their interest in the movement was social, cultural and literary' (Lewis 1968: 351). Although the extensive influence of the Young Turk movement had started deteriorating after 1918, its impact was deeper and longer lasting. Its ideals had given rise to a number of such movements and its name came to be applied to any radical or rebellious group within any party or organization outside Turkey.

In Turkey, a series of reforms from Lala Dauri, Khat-i Sharifi, Gulkhana, Tanzimat, etc., were already in vogue. Ismail Gaspiranski's famous movement called the 'Jadid' movement, started spreading not only in Turkey but also from there to Central Asia. Like all its sister organizations elsewhere the Jadid movement too was seen, suspected, misunderstood and at times appreciated and followed zealously since it originated in complex circumstances. The *Usuli Jadid* schools, study circles, group discussions changed the scenario and individuals like Ismail Gaspiranski, Abdul Rashid Ibrahim and Sadr Nizamovich Maqsud and a number of other lesser known but sincere Tartar reformists were the first to initiate the Jadid movement in Central Asia. They visited Ashkabad, Bukhara, Samarqand, Khoqand and Tashkent spreading new messages. The Jadid movement had first started in Turkistan and then engulfed Bukhara and Khiva (1907) gathering momentum after the Young Turk Revolution (1908-9). Suffice it to say that in addition to the direct influence of Tartar national elements, the Young Turks of Turkey, the Turkic national bourgeoise within the Russian Empire, the influence over them of emergence of nationalism in Persia, India and Egypt cannot altogether be ignored. The liberal Constitution Revolution in Persia (1905-9) and the Young Turk movement of

Turkey (1908) had as much an impact on the Revolutionary Jadids of Central Asia as the Turkish paper *Sirat-i Mustaqim*, the Indian paper *Hubb al-Watan*, and the Persian paper *Habl al-Matim*. The constant exchange of ideas among various countries in the region naturally assisted in forging the leadership of the new brands.

In Afghanistan, the reign of Amir Habibullah is said to be the watershed when seeds (if not full-scale) of modernization, liberalization of the political system and large-scale reforms transformed the socio-political scenario there. When flocks of exiles from Afghanistan were herded back to their motherland bubbling with new ideas, one of them, Mahmud Tarzi, who had received his education in the Ottoman Empire where Ismail Gaspranski's movement had gathered momentum, also came and set the scene for reforms. As the Chairman of a translation bureau of the Afghan Press, which dates from this period, he started publishing his own newspaper *Siraj al-Akhbari Afghanistan* (Lamp of the News of Afghanistan) with an advocacy of modern education reformist attitude and activities that earned for him both bouquets and brick bats. The matrimonial alliances with the ruling family somehow protected Tarzi despite the 'Veiled criticism of Habibullah's government for injustice, social inequalities and ignorance in Afghanistan' (Magnus 1998/2000: 39-40). Gradually these Young Afghans managed to penetrate into the ruling clique. Already the presence of Tarzi (as Foreign Minister and Chief Adviser on Kabul's domestic policies, educational and modernization issues during the reign of his (Tarzi's) own son-in-law king Amanullah) and a coterie the ruling elite was bound to boomerang upon the state of Amir Habibullah who 'paid with his life for his policies' (Magnus 1998/2000: 39). How strong was the influence of these strategists on the king can be gauged from the fact that their dream of a constitutional monarchy, a 'new culture' for Afghanistan and anti-imperialist policy, soon goaded him (Amanullah) to take the deadly step of including their ideas into his first constitution. But this appeasing policy could hardly satisfy the diehard modernists section of the Young Afghans, some of whom were so keen to establish a Republic after overthrowing Amanullah that they formed a *Hizb-i Niqabdar* (veiled party)—a secret organization. Much to the chagrin of Amanullah who even failed to satisfy the conservative section who rejected the proposal altogether and branded it as the 'handwork of communism and not of Islam' (Magnus 1998/2000: 44). Even during the Musahiban rule of forty-five years, such was the impact of the Young brother and Afghan movement that a Young Afghan student in Germany assassinated the king's brother—the Afghan Ambassador to Berlin (Magnus 1998/2000: 100).

For Amanullah, however, this was the death-knell of his monarchy in 1929 and he bided his time as an exile in Rome. The monarchy remained in the hands of Nadir Shah till his assassination in 1933. Under Shah Mahmud Khan Ghazi, the prime minister after the Second World War, the movement took a more active turn. The broad-based and widely supported party known as 'the Awakened Youth' (*Wishi Zalmayan*) was founded in 1947 under whose banner the revolutionary and reformists activities of liberal groups continued. At this stage, the newspaper *Nida-ye Khalq* (Voice of the Masses) was started by Abdul Rahman Mahmudi who established a political party Khalq (Masses), whose base and strength were the students of Kabul University, which proves that the Young Afghan movement of the early twentieth century had left its strong influence and impact upon Afghanistan. It has rightly been pointed out that 'the groups and individuals associated with the "liberal Seventh Parliament" period formed a bridge joining the era of the Young Afghans of the 1920s, the partisans of "New Democracy" in the 1964 constitution, and the Marxist of the 1970s' (Magnus 1998/2000: 100-2).

Japan too had its own share of the Young movement. Although the need for reform was felt by the Japanese in the nineteenth century, we hear of 'Youngs', as early as 1615-16 in Tokugawa, Japan. Like many other eastern states, there was the Tokugawa Shogunate also in which the senior ones called the 'Elders' comprised four to six larger house *daimyos* who had authority over the national affairs and were members of the older council. There was a junior council 'house daimyo called "Young Elders" who had the charge of [the] Shogun's bannermen and lesser retainers, etc. In 1825 Aizawa Seishisai (1782-1863) [in] the document called *New*

Proposals had persuaded the shogunate to smash the 'barbarian whenever they come in sight'. The Meiji leaders had 'experimented with a Shinto Programme and Shinto Department (*Jingikan*) in the new Western style government' that was set up early in 1808. The restructuring of the government in 1869 which provided a high pedestal to the Shinto Department at the same level as the Council of State, and rejuvenated the Shinto ideology and missionaries, gradually paved the way for restoration and educational reforms. It was a stage when the Japanese too, like others in Asia, decided that 'knowledge shall be sought from all over the world and thus shall strengthen the foundations of the "Imperial" national polity (*Kokutai*). There was the government's "drive for the economic expansion and increase in production" with the current slogan of *Fukoku Kyohei* (rich country - strong army) (Brown 1955: 91-105). The Kodo group mainly comprised the younger field officers and the radicals in the military, who gave vent to their belligerent attitude by killing their political targets in 1930-4 and organizing coups. They were assisted in this task by the civilian population (Hunter 1989: 277-9).

Kodoha (Young Officer's Group) was a radical group, aspiring for a 'reorganization of society which would eliminate the power of financial political party, and bureaucratic cliques so that Japan would have greater power for fulfilling her national mission'. The *Toseiha* (control group) which held high positions and followed

direct action tactics and thereby strengthened the hands of army in the internal and external affairs of the country until 1933, agreed with the Kodoha in realizing the importance of giving the army a more responsible role in the affairs of the state. In 1934, one of the several pamphlets issued at that time created a serious controversy. It was entitled *Kokubo no Hongi to Sono Kyoko no Teisho* (Principles of national defence and proposal for strengthening them).

Accordingly, issues pertaining to human welfare were taken up from the causes of poverty to problems of defence—and each was analysed (Brown 1955: 195-9, 202, 235). The control group felt the danger as early as 1932 and resorted to transfer and reshuffling of military officers to 'weaken the influence of the more radical young officers'. But this attitude ignited the radical *Kodoha* who organized rebellions but to no avail as they were gradually suppressed to an extent that either they committed suicide or surrendered (Brown 1955: 195-9, 202, 235).

There were two phases of this Young movement starting from 1919 and concluding in 1939. The first phase was when civilians dominated. The period from 1931 onwards heralded the ascendancy of the militarists. Although they were in power, the hall-mark of the period continued to be internal reforms. It is surmised that during the first phase there were international interest which superseded and 'overshadowed' nationalism which remained at its lowest ebb, while in the second phase national interests were paramount (Brown 1955: 195-9, 202, 235).

In China also, the reform and modernizing movements had started with the title 'Young' (*East Asia* 1998: 740, 773, 882, 942). There was the movement *La Jeunesse* (New Youth) established by a 'revolutionary journalist' Ch'en Tu-'hsiu from a prosperous family who completed his studies in Japan and France and was not only a passive observer but an active participant in the political revolution of 1911. He had zealously advocated individual freedom and the ideas of the French Revolution 'Liberty, Equality and Fraternity'. Chien edited a newspaper *New Youth* (*East Asia* 1998: 767-8, 773).

The intellectual activities from 1919-22 gave impetus to a new political and cultural association—the 'New Culture Movement' in China. Since nationalism and anti-imperialism were thought to be synonymous and there was an attack on Confucianism, 'doubts on antiquity' and 'pragmatic approach' to 'problems' which were to be 'analysed' by the 'genetic method' and with a critical attitude.

In China the reform movements and processed modernization started in the final decade of the monarchy. The phase of reforms during the Ching regime (1901-11) was described as 'less a period of collapse than of new beginning' when new schools were opened, new scholars also emerged.

The abolition of the 'Eight legged essay' and the conversion of the old academies (*shu yuan*) into government schools, new armies, rise of Yuan Shih Kai, administrative reforms, restructuring of Peking's financial reforms, which seemed to menacingly endanger many 'rice bowls' but finally came out with a national budget in which central and provincial government revenues were differentiated from those of local railway construction.

By 1911 the provincial assemblies and the press provided a forum for both the 'gentry' interests and new class of young students and military officers—'Young China'. When the Communists International (established in March 1919) invoked to organize the first communist party in China, it was also the time when the workers and students who mostly hailed from Hunan, in 1921 succeeded in establishing their own 'Young China' Communist Party in Paris of which Chou En Lai became the leader following the All China Federation of Trade Unions established in 1922. Several other associations and organizations sprang up like the 'Democratic Youth' (34 million in 1947) and for the students and scholars an organization called the 'Young Pioneers' (*East Asia* 1998: 726, 740, 773, 882, 942).

In Vietnam also, a 'Vietnamese Revolutionary Youth League' was formed in which young Vietnamese were recruited. The newspaper published by them was also called *Thanh Nien* (Youth) (*East Asia* 1998: 882).

Another dimension of these Young movements was said to be a socio-religious reassertion when these Western educated Buddhists used religion as a rallying point for resistance to colonialism. A number of Young Men's Buddhist Societies sprang up and their missionary activists were in full swing there 'to meet Christianity on its own ground' (Vinacke 1982: 293, 322). There was the Young Men's Buddhist Society formed in China which was engaged in social welfare, though the revival of Buddhism 'was merely in its beginning in 1931' (Tarling 1992: 286). In Formosa and other places also, a number of Buddhist Young Men's Associations were organized. Although the Japanese Buddhism had engrossed itself in the day-to-day problems of their followers but it was yet to evolve its code of morality in a big way which could be useful for the modern social structure (Vinacke 1982: 293, 322). The Young Men's Buddhist Association in South-East Asia (though deriving from some small localized precursor) had emerged with obvious echoes of the West's Young Men's Buddhist Association. In Burma, the early modernist and nationalist activities had their roots in religion and an upsurge of such Young Men's Buddhist Association was initiated in 1906. In the beginning these were nonpolitical bodies focused on cultural and religious bases. However, these became politicized by 1910. The ecclesiastical origins of the organization sustained it and gave it ample opportunities to raise 'formidable strategic issues on which to challenge colonial authority' (Tarling 1992: 125, 286-7, 302-3, 572-3). From this humble origin emerged a new umbrella organization—the General Council of Burmese Associations. It is surmised that since Sangha was weakened, lay movements like Young Men's Buddhist Association grew stronger and became the 'visible foci of anti-colonial resistance' and 'religious issues remained prominent within political nationalism'. The principles of Buddhism too had to be refashioned in the light of Western modern standards. Neither the Young Men's Buddhist Association was 'traditionalist nor antiquarian' as it was led by the 'educated and Anglicized elite' which had further paved the way for political and more meaningful reforms (Cady 1964: 403-4, 506-7).

Modernist and reform movements in the Malay peninsula having its main thrust on religion and education started in 1940. They were also inspired by the reformists of Middle East and Turkey. As in the Netherlands East Indies and elsewhere there were two groups: *kaum tua* (elder group) against whose conservatism the reformist *kaum muda* (young group) started its activities perhaps in 1926. When the anti-Japanese trend engulfed the Chinese arena, the activities of the apprehensive Malays increased. Consequently in 1937, the branches of Singapore, Malay Union dotted Melaka and the Penang and Malay Association was formed. A radical Kesatuan Melayu Meda or Malay Youth Union—a branch of an informal student group at the Sultan Idris Training College was established. They were indifferent to the issues of non-cooperation, opposition to British imperialism and loyalty to the Sultan and concentrated upon promoting nationalism and educating the lower classes who formed its main constituent basis for strength and power (Tarling 1992: 302-3).

The Indonesians too had established a 'Young Muslim League'

and started their 'preaching missions' (Cady 1964: 377, 524, 571).

In India, such 'new' and 'Young' movements had started in different forms and at different levels and places but with the same aim and goal and due to the same reasons. Bengal, however, was the foremost centre of such movements. Amvica C. Majumdar's comment that: 'As Europe is unthinkable without France, so India would be unthinkable without Bengal' may sound to be a bit chauvinistic but there is some grain of truth in it. Lala Lajpat Rai also observed in *Young India* that 'what was done in Bengal found its echo in the rest of the country'. Keshub Chandra Sen (1838-84), actively engaged in his reform activities had organized the 'Sangit Sabha' or 'Association for Mutual Improvement' in 1860. His 'undiminished' energy and extraordinary imaginative mind exhibited itself in the publication of several pamphlets, one of which was entitled 'Young Bengal, This is for You' (Gordon 1964: 25-34, 85, 89-92). Various organizations like the British Indian Association (founded in 1851), Indian Association (founded in 1876), and the Bengal Contingents in the Indian National Congress and Ameer Ali's Central National Mohammedan Associations comprised the urban educated—the so-called and self-styled 'middle class' for whom elitist interests were paramount in determining their attitudes and pattern of policies. By 1870 this allied contingent of urban elite was exposed and had to face challenges from young men like Surendranath Bannerjea, Sisir Kumar Ghosh and others (Gordon 1964: 25-34, 85, 89-92; Shastri 1972: 156-7). Bannerjea had established a more efficacious and practically sound 'New Indian Association' to speak for all. Bannerjea's autobiography *A Nation in Making*, emphasized his modern ideas, 'sympathy for the poor' and 'hatred for sordid means'. Since Bannerjea was a follower of Burke, he believed in a 'positive relationship between generations and a continuity tradition'. He is said to have likened himself to Mazzini raising a fallen and degraded Italy. When there was the division in the movement, the cleavage further sharpened and the 'most celebrated split' occurred between the moderates and the extremists, the latter calling themselves as 'the New Party'. Due to its belligerence, the party soon faced large-scale imprisonment of its leaders (Gordon 1964: 25-34, 85; Shastri 1972: 56-7).

There was the Young Men's Christian Association which originally confined its activities to the welfare of Christians but which later started reaching out to Indians in 1889. Social service became a part of the Young Men's Christian Association and Hindus zealously worked for it. Gradually, the newly awakened sense of patriotism and pride in their own identity had so intensely overtaken the Indians that a series of such Associations started coming up. There was a new version of Young Men's Buddhist Association and then in imitation there sprang up a Young Men's Sikh Association in Lahore and a Khalsa Young Men's Association in Amritsar with their own newspaper, *The Khalsa Young Men's Magazine* (Farquhar 1977: 25, 423, 80, 125, 278, 329, 343, 444). The proposal to constitute a 'Young Men's Indian Association' was said to be confessedly 'in imitation' of the Young Men's Christian Association constituted primarily for the purpose of saving young men from Christian influence'. The purpose was to establish a secular organization (Farquhar 1977: 278). It is generally assumed that Keshub Chandra Sen and his new religious movement 'had hitherto caught the imagination of Young Bengal'. Sinha categorically mentions that

> there is no doubt that it was mainly due to Surendra Nath that the attention of Young Bengal was diverted from the field of religion and social reform to patriotism and political organization. He inspired the young students by his lectures on Joseph Mazzini and the Young Italy movement. By his wonderful eloquence, he vividly drew the picture of Italy's misery under Austrian domination, which could not fail to evoke in the minds of his audience the similar condition of India under the British rule.

In the fiery speech delivered by him in 1878, he infused a new spirit among the youth and exhorted them to 'dedicate their lives for the good of their country, and laid special emphasis on the unity among different communities' (Sinha 1967: 164, 208, 215, 399-404, 406, 417, 453).

With the emergence of the New Bengal movements, a new chapter began.

> The followers of Henry Louis Derozio were collectively known as the Young or New Bengal, the term being also used for the movement they initiated. Variously criticized as anglicists and atheists, these young men were in reality,

idealists in search of utopia. They were the men in whom the nationalist movement first manifested itself, their major contribution lay in the impetus they gave to free and national thinking and a spirit of inquiry that was the hallmark of the age of reasons. (Mehra 1977: 90-1)

Swami Vivekananda's preaching emphasized the significance of 'muscles of iron and nerves of steel inside in which dwells a mind of the same material as that of which the thunderbolt is made.' Strength, manhood *kshatriya virya brahma tejah*. In a lecture delivered before an assembly of the Young Bengalis, he said, 'In order to march boldly in equal pace side by side with other materially advanced nations of the world, Young Bengal, emulate the manly ways of Lakshmi Bai—imitate the virtues of other nations, cultivate their technical skills and qualities of life and then with a modern standard of morale and efficiency attained, pay them, the foreign usurpers in their own coins in your own country to unfasten the alien octopus hold on the citadel of oriental culture' (Sinha 1967: 406-17, 453). After acquiring advanced English education with all its concomitants, the students of Hindu College founded in 1817 an organization called the 'Young Bengal' comprising an enlightened group of 'highly mixed phenomenon'. It is surmised that 'Young Bengal read Tom Paine, admired revolutionary France, hated the British Tories, wrote poems about the fallen state of the motherland and dreamt of a free and self-governing India in the future'. Many of the Young Bengal members were closely linked with the Bengal British India Society, established by George Thompson in 1843 (Sinha 1967: 406-17, 453). This 'new social force' had given birth to a tug of war, a cultural schism and confrontation, between the upholders of conservatism and tradition on the one hand and the believers in transformation, the 'isolated' group of 'Young Bengal', on the other (Sinha 1967: 399, 401). Assisted by the increasing significance of English education which simultaneously created a 'middle class society' (paving the way for a transition from the orthodoxy to heterodoxy) and a slow transfer from *bari* (village homes) to *basha*, which overthrew the shackles of 'traditional rule of commensality' (Sinha 1967: 406, 417).

There were many newspapers, e.g. the *Bengal Spectator*, *Parthenon*, *Hesperus Inquirer*, *Quil*, *Gyaneveshwar*, *Hindu Pioneer*, etc., through which were transmitted the new ideas about various aspects of social change (Mehra 1985: 90, 91). The important members who were actively involved in the Young Bengal movement included men like Krishnamohan Bandyopadhyay, Rasik Krishna Malik, Radhanath Shiqdar, Dakshina Ranjan Mukhopadhyay, Peary Chand Mittra and Ramtanu Lahiri (Mehra 1985: 90, 91).

When Bal Gangadhar Tilak explained 'Swaraj', in Calcutta, in the following pragmatic words: 'I want to have the key of my house, and not merely one stranger turned out of it,' the fundamental difference over methods and the question of how to confront the colonialists and how to go about it was bothering the young and the old alike. The inexperienced but enthusiastic approach led to the formation of Upadhyay's *Sandhya* and Bipin Chandra Pal's *New India* in 1906.

The 'passive resistance' is said to have 'acquired its finished form through the writings of Bipin Chandra along with Aurobindo during 1906-7. While the Swadeshi movement was continuing and in quick succession to Lipton's godown strikers' protest, there was the Barisal settlement office clerk's strike against increased hours of work wherein not only 63 were dismissed but victimization of others also followed. It was at this juncture that the *New India* of Bipin Chandra Pal goaded people to adopt the 'Russian methods of self-defence'. 'If two or three thousand clerks simultaneously struck work by way of protest against the dismissal for sixty-three of their brethren, it would bring even the Fuller Government to its knees' (Sarkar 1973: 68, 205, 256, 260, 263, 265). The abuses showered on Fuller invited the wrath of the British who wanted the prosecution of *New India*, giving 'a long rope down to the middle of 1907'. Bipin Chandra Pal's *New India*, the only English language weekly launched in August 1901, had a circulation of about 1,500 in 1908. From August 1906, *Bande Matram* had also been preaching 'nationalism'. All the newspapers and national press were 'Shackled', when in June 1908 the Newspapers (Incitement to offences) Act VII of 1908 was enunciated (Sarkar 1973: 68, 205, 256, 260, 263, 265).

The Arya Kumar Sabha or Young Men's Arya Association, a

replica of the Young Men's Christian Association, was also organized. The Digambaras sect also held its first yearly meeting in 1893 and subsequent to this conference within one year to eighteen months a 'Jain Young Men's Association' was established, which was later on renamed the 'All India Jain Association' (or Bharata Jain Mahamandala) with its office at Lucknow. Subsequently, in 1903, the Shvetambara sect organized a conference and Sthanakavasis constituted their group. Originally, the objectives of the Association was the union and progress of the Jain community and the propagation of Jainism (Farquhar 1977: 278-9, 334, 343). Gradually a Young Men's Sikh Association in Lahore and a Khalsa Young Men's Association in Amritsar were also launched on the same pattern of Young Men's Christian Association and a paper *The Khalsa Young Men's Magazine* also began to be published.

The Young movements had flourished in the Asian region when the period of 'Imperialism of free trade' and the colonizing schemes had reached its apex not only in Europe but in India and other places as well. Large scale conquests and external and internal plunder as a result of British expansionist policies had increased the political and financial power of the mother country and expanded its empire to an expanse which had the difference of sunrise and sunset. The period of boom from 1808 to 1888 had gradually subsided but the anger and resentment which had escalated by the high-handedness of imperialist masters never came down. The British disaster in Afghanistan had given the first blow to the invincibility of the imperialists. Japan's victory in 1905 further raised the hopes of the struggling Asians. The reformist and revivalist movements and religious and cultural transformations were symptomatic of a defiance of alien powers usurping the Asian lands and its rich resources. From the early twentieth century, an upsurge of these Young movements had, therefore, started changing the political and socio-economic scenario. Soviet historians claim that 'the 1905 revolution was largely responsible for the rise of progressive national liberation movements' including the Young movement in Afghanistan and that the 1905 revolution played the same role in Asia as the French Revolution had played in Europe in goading the Ottoman Empire, Persia, China, Mongolia, India and Afghanistan.

Gregorian, however, thinks that the Young Afghan movement perhaps received an impetus from the Anglo-Russian Convention of 1907, which directly threatened Afghan independence. The fears of the Asian nationalists are well-expressed through the Persian poet Bahar in his poem 'A Critical Tribute to Sir Edward Grey':

Alas that thou for all thy wits, has wrought
A deed which, save regret, can yield thee naught
For India's gates, closed for a hundred years,
To Russians now you open without fears,
Not Persian only feels the Russian squeeze
Tis felt by Afghans and by Kashgaris.

The Persian newspaper *Habl-al Matin* published in Calcutta wrote: 'the Russian and the English governments will grant each other opportunities for commercial activities. What right have Russians on Persia to grant or not grant—that which belongs to us? We are not so youthful as to want a protector, and we are not mad or insane and hence in need of one . . .' (Gregorian 1969: 208-13). The Persians, Young Turks, Chinese revolutionaries and subsequently the *Mashroutyat* movement (constitutional movement) in Afghanistan, and Young movements in India, Japan and other places had largely been given an impetus by the 'intellectual currents and by a number of external events like the Russo-Japanese War, the Constitutional Revolution in Iran (1905-9), the Ottoman Empire and China (1906-11), the spread of pan-Islamism, the Italo-Turkish (1911) and Balkan wars (1912-13), [the] First World War, the Russian Revolution and the proclamation of Wilson's Fourteen Points' (Gregorian 1969: 165). The result was a religious and cultural sense of identity which may not have been a 'consciously articulated feeling' initially but an undercurrent linking subcontinental South Asia. This sort of linkages brought people in contact with each other and with the administrative processes which unified continental geo-strategic nature and contributed to the emergence of a collective political identity through technology and economic advancement—a by-product of imperialism. Inferiority complex was replaced by a sense of discovery about the richness of their past, which cannot be forgotten and should become a part of reassertion.

A general survey of these Young movements shows that though these ideas have been borrowed from the West, each region had adapted and adopted it in its own indigenous form. Almost the entire Asia had experienced a similar kind of reawakening, a rising sense of religious and cultural identity—a sense of renaissance. Some of these Young movements drew inspiration and sustenance initially from the Young Ottoman and Young Turk movements. The Young Turk movement proved to be a political catalyst which enthused and goaded the Asians to fight for their rights against the colonialists. The desire for and the subsequent emergence of a collective identity was a direct result of the resentment and suppressed anger which took the form of reassertion—a by-product of the humiliating treatment meted out to the Asians. There was a scintillating consciousness of their own grand past and rich cultural heritage—the realization of which had dawned upon the Asians, reassuring them that their past was not without meaning and that they were something and they must become something.[3]

NOTES

1. For example, the Babist Revolt (1844-52) in Persia; the Taiping Revolution (1851-64) in China; Revolt of 1857 in India.
2. In 1905 and after, there were Persian Constitutional Revolution (1905-9); anti-British struggle by All-India National Congress (1905-8); the Turkish Revolution (1908-9) and the Chinese revolt against the Ching Dynasty (1911-12).
3. J.N. Dixit, delivering the Prof. Saiyid Nurul Hasan Memorial Lecture, at Aligarh Muslim University (n.d.).

REFERENCES

East Asia, *History of China and Japan* (Delhi: 1998).
Ahmad, Feroz, *Young Turks* (Oxford: 1969).
Brown, Delmer M., *Nationalism in Japan* (1955).
Cady, John F., *Southeast Asia: Its Historical Development* (1964).
Cleaveland, W.L., *A History of Modern Middle East* (Oxford: 1984).
Farquhar, J.N., *Modern Religious Movements in India* (New Delhi: 1977).

Gordon, Leonard A., *Bengal: The Nationalist Movement 1876-1940* (New York: 1964).
Gregorian, Vartan, *The Emergence of Modern Afghanistan* (Stanford: 1969),
Hunter, Janet E., *The Emergence of Modern Japan* (New York: 1989).
Isaacs, Harold (ed.), *The Tragedy of The Chinese Revolution* (Stanford: 1969).
Lewis, Bernard, *Emergence of Modern Turkey* (Oxford: 1968).
Magnus, Ralph H. and Eden Nabi, *Mullah, Marx and Mujahid: Afghanistan* (Oxford: 1998/2000).
Mehra, Parshotam, *A Dictionary of Modern Indian History (1707-1947)* (New Delhi: 1985).
Samson, *Japan: A Short Cultural History* (Harlow: 1963).
Sarkar, Sumit, *The Swadeshi Movement in Bengal* (New Delhi: 1973).
Shastri, Pandit Sivanath, *A History of the Renaissance in Bengal* (Calcutta: 1972).
Sinha, Narendra Krishna, *The History of Bengal (1757-1905)* (Calcutta: 1967).
Tarling, Nicholas, *The Cambridge History of Southern Asia* (Cambridge: 1992).
Vinacke, Harold M., *A History of the Far East in Modern Times* (Ludhiana: 1982).

CHAPTER 3

Jadid Movement in the Volga-Ural Region

NADIR DEVLET

HISTORICAL BACKGROUND

In the Volga-Ural region and western Siberia, when the Golden Horde state (1240-1502) started to disintegrate, new political institutions like the Kazan Khanate (1437-1552), Crimean Khanate (1460-1783), Astrakhan Khanate (1466-1556), Kasim Khanate (1445-1681) and Siberian Khanate (1460-1598) were established. In the beginning they created serious military threat to the Russian principalities. But the Russians under the leadership of the Moscow principality ultimately get the upper hand.

Ivan the fourth (Terrible), *kniaz* (prince) of Moscow principality, with the help of Western technology, was able to become the most powerful among the Russian principalities. The leadership ability of Moscow was undisputable and Ivan the Terrible decided to destroy his historical enemy, the Kazan Khanate. He used the conflicting parties of the khanate leadership cleverly for his purpose and in October 1552 he dealt a death blow to the Kazan Khanate. His victory was also at the same time a turning point in Russian history. Kazan Khanate was the main obstacle in the way of Russian advance along the Volga and to the Caspian Sea. It was situated at the Middle Volga. Having won Kazan Khanate, the Moscow principality turned from a national Russian state into a multinational imperialistic state. This success of Ivan the Terrible continued with the occupation of another Golden Horde Khanate, namely, Astrakhan, on the shores of the Caspian Sea, in 1556. Both victories gave Moscow the possibility and courage to expand its territories into the Caucasus (along the Terek River), into the Crimean peninsula (Azak fortress), the Urals and western

Siberia. Thus, in 1598, the third Golden Horde Khanate, Siberia, was annexed. Between the years of 1593 and 1604, Siberia was totally occupied. Also in 1604, the nomadic Nogai tribes, who were occupying the territory between Astrakhan and Crimean Khanates, had to accept the Russian domination.

Conquest of the Volga-Ural Region

After the conquest of the Kazan Khanate in 1552, every nation, ethnic group or tribe in the east, i.e. in the Volga-Ural region, Caucasus, Siberia and Central Asia was brought under the Russian domination one by one. The Russian expansion continued until the second half of the nineteenth century. Almost all the Turkic peoples, Ugric-Fins, Mongol nations, peoples of Caucasus, Armenians, Georgians, Siberian peoples, Tajiks, etc., became subjects of the Russian Empire. The Russian conquest of the Asiatic part of Turkic world, with the exception of eastern Turkestan, spanned approximately three centuries. In other words, the Tsarist Russian Empire had the third largest Muslim population in the world, surpassed only by the British Empire, especially India, and the Ottoman Empire. After the Orthodox Church, the Muslims were the largest religious group in Russia, with a population of 18 million in a total of 125 million. According to the 1879 census, the Russians consisted of 44.5 per cent of the total population (55.5 million). The people of Khanate Khiva and Bukhara, which were under Russian protection, were not included in this number (app. 4.5 million). Muslim population was found in all parts of Russia—the Volga-Ural region, Siberia, Central Asia (Turkestan), Crimea, and the Caucasus. In the main cities of European Russia there had always been large groups of Muslims, especially Kazan Tatars, who, like the people of Azerbaijan, were advanced materially and culturally.

In the beginning of Russian advance, Moscow followed a brutal policy against its non-Russians, especially Turkic Muslim, subjects. Under the Russian domination, the Turkic peoples of the Volga-Ural region lost not only their material possessions, but also almost their cultural identity. The new Russian administration confiscated all lands, personal property, and instituted a policy of converting their Muslim and non-Muslim animist subjects into Christianity. This policy was quite successful, among the Ugric-Fin and Turkic non-Muslim Chuvash, but not between Muslim Tatars and the Bashkirs. Only a few Turkic nobles converted to Christianity out of fear of losing their lives and privileges. Turkic (i.e. Tatar) names among Russian families of today are a good example of this conversion. The majority of the population, however, fought against this forcible conversion. The result was that many Muslims were executed or deported, while others simply left their homelands and emigrated. Even today in the neighbourhood of Kazan, the capital of Tatarstan, in some 50 km radius, not a single Tatar village is to be found.

As a result of the Russian conquest, cultural life began to decay over the course of two centuries. In the wake of reduced religious freedom and an active policy of baptizing, the Turkic peoples turned more and more to Islam and religious education as a means of preserving their cultural identity.

Russian Advance into the Caucasus (1783-1828)

In the nineteenth century, Caucasus were divided among separate nationalities and their small khanates or states. The first Russian advance into northern Caucasus started in the seventeenth century. But serious military operations started only in 1822 towards the north Caucasus. Russian forces started to squeeze Nogais and Adyges on Kuban. These and other northern Caucasians, who was Muslims, started to immigrate to Turkey. After the Crimean War (1853-6), the Circassians were deported. Alexander the second nominated General Prince Bariatinski to the region as Governor-General and sent military forces to Dagistan and Chechnya of 240,000 in strength. Only the legendary Avar Sheikh Shamil (1798-1871) was able to struggle against the Russians for almost 25 years. But in 1859 even he was forced to surrender. In other words, from this time onwards Russians were the only power in the region.

Southern Caucasus, which was ruled by the Persian Empire, shared the same fate. In 1783, Catherine II declared that the Kingdom of Georgia was now under Russian protection and after several decades, in 1801, came under the rule of Russia. The

Azeris consisted of several tiny khanates (Ganja Kuba, Baku, Zaki, Shirvan, Karabagh, etc.). Following consecutive wars with Iran, eventually all were occupied one by one between 1805 and 1822. With the Turkmenchai agreement on February 1828, Aras River became the border between Iran (Persia) and Russia.

Russian Advance into the Kazakh Steppes (1731-1840s)

Relations between the Kazakh khans and chiefs and the Russians started soon after Ivan the Terrible occupied Kazan Khanate (1552) and the banks of the Volga. After the occupation of western Siberia, the Russians founded the cities of Tümen, Tobol'sk, Tara and Tomsk, which were places on the trade route with the Kazakhs. Peter the Great had wanted to take over the gold mines in eastern Turkistan around Yarkend. A large military force started its mission from Tobol'sk in 1715. In 1716 a fortress was founded in Omsk and in 1718 was founded the fortress of Semipalatinsk.

Towards the middle of the eighteenth century, a strong Kalmuk (Oirat) state had formed in Jungaria. Part of the Kalmuks entered the territory of the Kazakhs. A large group attacked the Kazakh tribes in 1732. The Greater and Middle Horde Kazakhs were deprived of the best pastures along the Chu and Talas. Their herds were taken away which led to a great famine. The Lesser Horde realized that the way to avoid disaster was to seek Russian protection. After 1731, the Middle Horde also accepted Russian protection in 1740. In 1822 the Russian government abolished the khanate of the Middle Horde by decree. In 1824 the khan of the Lesser Horde was dismissed and the Middle Horde was divided into three regions. By the 1840s the whole of the Kazakh country was taken under Russian rule. There were some uprisings but without any success.

Russian Advance into Central Asia

After the fall of the Kazan Khanate in 1552 it was certain that Russia would expand towards the east and south until she met with resistance. The rapidly developing industry and capitalism in Russia in the middle of the nineteenth century would certainly have tried to find new fields of activity.

Diplomatic and commercial relations between Russia and Central Asia developed in the sixteenth and seventeenth centuries. Cotton and silk products of Turkistan, especially Persian lamb, had been a much favoured commodity in Russia for a long time. Western European products entered Bukhara through Russia, and the products of India and Afghanistan were sent to Russia and Turkestan. There were two main trade routes that connected Russia and Central Asia at the end of the eighteenth century. The oldest one reached the Caspian Sea via the Volga and then Khiva and Bukhara via Mangyshlak. The second route made connection with Orenburg via Tashkent and Jaxartes. There was also another route that reached Tashkent via Semipalatinsk and Kyzylyar (Petropavlovsk), passing through the Kazakh steppes. Tashkent became a commercial centre. Between 1801 and 1820 Russian trade with the khanates of Turkestan rose from 1 million to 4 million roubles. Within the same period the exports of Turkestan to Russia rose from 2 million to 6 million roubles. Between the years 1830 and 1840, British trade in Central Asia suddenly developed in competition with the Russians. The Russian government was suspicious of British activities and began sending commissions to study the situation in the Central Asian khanates. In 1834 a military base was established at Fort Novo-Alexandrovsk on the north-eastern coast of Caspian. In 1839 followed the Khiva expedition under General V. Perovsky. The Russians moved towards Central Asia in 1847 by building the fortress Raimsk (Aral'sk) at the Jaxartes. In 1853 General Perovsky captured Ak-Mesjid, a fort belonging to Kokand. After this, the way to Tashkent was open.

After the Crimean War and the Treaty of Paris (1856), the Russian government sent in 1858 Colonel Ignat'yev to Khiva and Bukhara. Internal problems and the war with Shaykh Shamil, which ended in 1864, delayed the occupation of Turkistan. During this time, because of the American Civil War, all imports of cotton from America had stopped, and Russian factories could only obtain cotton from Turkistan. General Chernyayev occupied Chimkent in September 1864. After a year, in the summer of 1865, a military force of 1,950 men and 12 guns under Chernyayev's command was attached. Russian total loss was 25 deaths and 89 wounded soldiers. Tashkent, with a population of 80,000 belonged to the Kokand Khanate. There were 30,000 soldiers and 63 guns in the city; but the soldiers lacked discipline as well as modern weaponry, and soon Tashkent was occupied in June 1865. In May 1866 the Russians took over the cities of Khojand and then Ura-Tübe. The entire area was annexed to Russia and a governor-general of Turkistan was established in 1867. General K.P. Kaufman (von Kauffman) was appointed governor-general. In 1868 Samarkand was taken. Further resistance was impossible for Bukhara, and Muzzafar al-Din signed a treaty, according to which Khojand, Ura-tübe, Jizak and Samarkand with their neighbouring lands were given to the Russians. After five years in 1873, a peace treaty was signed between Russia and Bukhara in which the latter accepted Russian protection. In 1874 the Trans-Caspian military district was formed. Khiva also ended in the same way. The city of Kokand was occupied, and the khanate was officially abolished in 1876 and the Russian province of Transcaspian was created. In 1877 the Russians started a military operation against Turkmens. The latter showed great resistance at Gök-Tepe on 15 January 1881 but the city of Merv fell in 1884 and Russian reached the borders of Afghanistan. In 1888 an Anglo-Russian Boundary Commission completed the demarcation of the border between Afghanistan and Russia, and the Russian advance in Central Asia came to an end.

The Spread of Islam

In the end of seventh century there was a huge spiritual, religious, cultural development in the Arab peninsula. This new spiritual force mobilized the Arabs so much so that they started to spread their religious, economic and political influence throughout the world. Even though Arab conquerors used force, Islam was propagated not so much by sword or the threat of force but by its civilization, material, cultural and spiritual achievements. The development of *madrasahs* (religious schools) strengthened the intellectual infrastructure of Islam. Undoubtedly, all these played a role in the process. Merchants and Sufis, who had knowledge of Islam, sacrificed their lives in propagating Islam everywhere. They were one of the key factors in the success of spreading Islam. The

Islamic influence was very big among the Turkic peoples. Volga Bulgars were the first among Turkic peoples who adopted Islam as their official religion in AD 922. They were far away from direct Arab influence, living in today's European part of Russia. But as sedentary people with a long tradition of trade, on the Volga and other nearby rivers which were the main water transport lines to Europe, Bulgars had connections also with Arab merchants. So the Bulgar ruler Khan Almas, after seeking the spread of Islam among his people decided to adopt Islam officially. Certainly in his decision there were also some political intentions. Maybe, the primary intention was to please his people. But the second and most important aim was to get aid from Muslim rulers against his enemies, the Slavs, who were becoming a serious threat to the Volga Bulgar state. But his hopes in that respect were dashed because the Abbasid Caliph did not provide any material help to build fortresses or give him new weaponry but just helped in building mosques and sending religious scholars to teach Islam. However the official recognition of Islam continued and the Bulgars became Muslims.

Islam was propagated not so much by the sword or the threat of force (although this was not absent), as by its civilization, material, cultural and spiritual achievements. The Karakhanids were the first in Central Asia to adopt Islam as their official religion. Merchants and Sufis were one of the key factors in the success of Islam here. The Eurasian nomads, having been exposed to a variety of universal religions and adopted several of them (e.g. Manichaeism and Buddhism among the Uighurs, and Judaism, Christianity and Islam among the Khazars), were familiar with the fundamental notions of the monotheistic faiths of the Mediterranean world.

Islam had a long tradition in the Volga-Ural region. The famous religious scholar and historian Mardjani states in his work *Mustafad al-Akhbar fi Akvali Kazan va Bulgar* that the Bulgars adopted Islam in the period of Abbasid Caliph al-Mumin (813-33). Also, the well-known Orientalists I. Marquart, V.V. Barthold, A. Yu. Yakubovski, and A.E. Khalikov believe that Islam was introduced to Bulgars via Central Asia before the first half of the nineteenth century (Khalikov 1991: 48). Already approximately 70 years before the Russians adopted Christianity as their official religion (AD 989), Islam had been recognized as the state religion by the then Turkic Bulgar state.

Disappearance of Islam

Following his conquest, Ivan the terrible had mosques destroyed or converted into Orthodox churches. About 300,000–400,000 Tatar-Bashkirs were killed during the first years of the conquest and in 15 years, 206 villages and 60 large landed properties, the inhabitants of which were driven away, fell into Russian hands. Before the Russian invasion, the city of Kazan had 40,000 inhabitants, afterwards they numbered only 6,000 (Devlet 1998; 1999: 15). The Russian State supported the arbitrary actions of the Orthodox Church, which lasted for more than 200 years and, among other things, forced Muslims to be baptized. In the year 1756 in the *gubernia* (province) of Kazan, 418 out of the existing 536 mosques were destroyed; in the *gubernia* of Tobolsk 15 out of 113 and in the *gubernia* of Astrakhan 29 out 40. Until 1759, the Volga Tatars were not permitted to build mosques and *madrasahs*. (Devlet 1986: 336).

As mentioned earlier, the first few decades of the annexation of the peoples of Volga-Ural region was extremely terrible. After the occupation of the Kazan Khanate, the Russian administration acted very brutally. Thousands of Tatars were massacred. Most of the mosques, libraries, and historical buildings were destroyed, and Muslim inhabitants of the city of Kazan were largely deported. In the first years of Russian rule, some 350,000-400,000 people were killed. We don't have the exact figures, but it is estimated that in the middle of the seventeenth century in the region there were 77,000 mosques and 1.2 million Muslims. However, the Russian rule was not accepted so easily and there were a few revolts, the last one being in 1896-7.

One of the almost effective policies of the Russian administration was baptizing Muslims. The Tatars who accepted the conversion were given the same privileges as Russians and to Tatar nobles who became Christians were given the same privileges as the Russian nobles. But the Russian Orthodox Church was not utterly satisfied with such developments. For example, in the last quarter of the sixteenth century, Mitropolit Germogen complained that the new converts were living with Chuvashs, Cheremish (Chirmish or Mari) and Vot (Votiak or Udmurt) who didn't accept Christianity, did not go to the church, did not wear crosses and did not have icons in their houses, did not baptize their children and buried their dead in Tatar cemeteries. As a consequence of this report the Russian government gave orders to register all new converts and separate them from the non-Christians. Those who did not obey these orders were put in jail, beaten up yoked or chained. These severe measures were certainly effective. But even so, the number of converts was not as large as the Russian church had desired. For example, in 1763 in the Kazan government out of 110,264 Tatars only 13,615 accepted to become Christians. The Russian state supported the arbitrary actions of the Orthodox Church, which lasted for more than two hundred years. The Russian policy against Islam can be seen also in the destruction of mosques. In 1756 in Kazan out of 536 mosques 418 had been destroyed and Muslims were forbidden to build new ones. The same harsh pressure policy was followed against Tatar merchants and the rural population.

In the Pugachev revolt (1773-4), the Tatar-Bashkirs played an important role, but the majority remained loyal to the regime. This fact gave an idea to Catherine II to reward her Muslim subjects in some way. The other was that the Russian interest in Central Asia was increasing and Tatar merchants who showed ability in trading and who were also Muslims, and understood the local languages could be used as middlemen. Also the Tatar *mullahs* loyal to Russia could play an influential role among Kazakh-Kyrgyz nomads. Catherine II's first step was to allow the creation of a Tatar city assembly in Kazan, near the Russian one in 1782. The second step was to return the rights of the Tatar nobles who didn't accept conversion in 1784.

Recognition of Islam by the Russian State

The year 1788 was a turning point for the Muslims of the Volga-Ural region, because Catherine II adopted a more liberal policy towards her Muslim subjects and ordered to establish 'The Religious Administration' (*Dukhovnoe Sobrania—Orenburg Makhkama-i Sharriya*) in Ufa. This consisted of a *mufti* acting as the chairman and nine administrative officials, their main duty was to examine and appoint the religious leaders requested by the Muslim congregation. Even this administration functioned as a controlling organ to the state, at the same time it was representing the official recognition of Islam by the Russian State.

Kazan, Orenburg, Ufa, Samara, Simbir, Saratov, Penza, Perm, Tambov, Astrakhan, Viatka, Tobolsk and Tomsk were under the jurisdiction of this Religious Administration. In the 1870s the Religious Administration registered 2,074,182 Muslims, 3,750 mosques and 1,569 *madrasahs* (Merdjani 1989: 210). According to the journal *Shura*, in 1881 for the 16 million Muslims there were approximately 16,000 district schools (*mahala maktabs*) and 213 *madrasahs*. In these institutions approximately half a million pupils were educated (*Tarbiye wa talim* 1912: 274-5). But the majority of these *madrasahs* consisted of only one classroom, which was semi-detached to the mosque, and the instructions was given by the *mullah* of the same mosque. Usually the local language 'Turki' was not taught.

But the Russian Orthodox Church in the meantime had done some missionary work among the native, non-Russian populace under the pretext of protecting the state, though the results, however, did not live up to their expectations; the Tatars particularly rejected these conversion attempts. At the fifth census taken in 1796, 103,050 male and 108,290 female Tatars lived in the *gubernia* of Kazan, only 13,384 men and 13,922 women were baptized (Glazik 1959: 112).

Revival of Islam

After Catherine II's reforms, *mullahs* no longer received their higher education in Bukhara, but in Istanbul, Cairo or Madina. In 1868, already 729 mosques existed in the Kazan *gubernia* and the number rose from year to year. The spiritual works of the *mullahs* produced good results. In Nizhni-Novgorod, in 1802, the Tatar Christians (*Kreshen*) openly abandoned Christianity (Glazik

1959: 114). The Orthodox Church was extremely alarmed by this fact and missionaries like the famous Ilminskii (1822-91) adopted diverse measures to keep the baptized Tatars in church. Among other things, 1,599,385 copies of Christian religious writings in 20 different languages were published from 1867 to 1899. These attempts, however, could not stop the return to Islam (Glazik 1959: 141-2).

Publishing Activities

The Muslims, at the same time, had not been inactive. Since printing in Arabic script had been allowed, they began reproducing mainly religious literature and distributing it among the population. From 1801 to 1855, 577 books were printed in Kazan. From 1842 to 1852, 23,600 copies of the Koran and 44,300 copies of *Haftiyak* (seventh part of the Koran) were printed; and from 1853 to 1859, 82,300 copies of the Koran and 165,000 of the *Haftiyak* were printed (Devlet 1998: 16). The Muslims tried not only to become active in printing but also in opening new mosques and *maktab-madrasahs.*

Maktab-Madrasahs

In the Volga-Ural region the *mullahs* organized the religious education and the Russian Ministry of Education preferred not to interfere. Until the end of the nineteenth century, in every big Muslim village or settlement near a mosque, a *maktab* functioned in order to give the children religious education. The teachers of such educational institutions were *mullahs* and therefore the curriculum was concentrated mainly on teaching how to read the Koran and religious rules. In some places, even the wives of *mullahs* (*abystai*) taught the village girls how to read and introduced some religious subjects.

Until the first half of the nineteenth century, the young generation of Tatar-Bashkirs who were cut-off from the official Russian education system searched for knowledge in Central Asia (Khiva, Bukhara, Samarkand, etc.). But at that time the education standard has already dropped and the *madrasahs* became scholastic, backward places. Personalities like Abdunnasir Kursavi (1771/1772-1812) or Shahabeddin Marjani (1818-89) who had their higher education in Central Asia recognized the low standard of such *madrasahs* and believed that some kind of reform had to be introduced in order to bring the Muslims into the educational level of the Russians. After returning to their country they started to propagate these kinds of ideas among the Muslims, which later led to the *jadid* (renaissance) movement (Kanlidere 1997: 198).

Economic Development among the Muslims

Catherine II's reform also allowed the Tatars to do more and more business. Because of their long tradition in trade, the Tatar merchants became successful. They were trading in grain, leather, soap, honey, wax, lumber, timber, cotton, fabric, textile, etc. These kinds of goods were sold to from Moscow, St. Petersburg, Arkhangelsk, Astrakhan, Orenburg, Don, to Ukraine, Ural, Siberia, Central Asia and Iran. By the end of the eighteenth century in Kazan there were 2,876 registered merchants, of which 2,015 were Russians and 861 Tatars. In other words 25 per cent were Muslim merchants.

Among the Tatars there were also manufacturers and industrialists. In 1781 in Kazan there was only one leather manufacturer. In 1812 the number of Tatar leather manufacturers grew up to 18 and they were producing half of the total Russian production. In 1854 there were 13 soap factories in Kazan, and ten of them belonged to Tatars. The third main industry was textiles and approximately 50 per cent of the total of Russian textile production was under the supervision of the Tatars. But competition with Russians was not easy, because government pressure in the economic field was also tremendous.

Another example of Russian political, economical and even social pressure can be seen in the decision of Peter the Great. In January 1678 he gave orders to establish a dockyard (*admiralstvo*) in Kazan. The necessary timber was cut and brought by a special forced labour called *lashman*. For this forced labour, in the beginning 56,000 Tatars were nominated. In the eighteenth century their number climbed to 109,000. Also Tatar-Bashkirs were drafted into the army and not pardoned like Central Asians. For them the military period was much longer than for an ordinary Russian, because they were sent to special camps to teach them Russian. In most cases they could be discharged from the army only on account of disability.

Jadidism among the Tatar-Bashkirs, Crimean Tatars and Azerbaijani Turks

Abdunnasir Kursavi (1771/72-1812) was among the first Tatar reformists. He had had his education in Bukhara and Samarkand, which were recognized in the past as the best centres for Islamic religious learning. But in his times these centres had already degenerated. Kursavi started with his criticism already when he was there and because of that he was sentenced to death, but had a lucky escape. After his return to his hometown he continued with his criticism. But the majority of *ishans* and *mullahs*, who had their higher education also in Bukhara, showed a resentment to this. After him, an Islamic scholar and maybe the first historian in the modern sense, Shahabeddin Marjani also started to criticize the scholastic, underdeveloped stand of education and archaic interpretations of the Koran. His ideas especially on education was published by his student and Tatar scholar Hussain Feyizkhani (1828-66), who accepted to the Kazan University, then elected to the Imperial Archaeological Society. The idea of reforming religious schools was first discussed in the work of Hussain Feyizkhani, called the *Islah-i Madaris* (Kanlidere 1997: 14). In his book he suggested introduction of non-religious subjects also in the curriculum of the *madrasa's* and to open a Tatar school according to European standards. Such ideas were practically organized by a Crimean intellectual Ismail Gasprinski. In this education system, practically the turning point was when Ismail Gasprinski opened his *usul-i savtiya* or *usul-i jadid* school in 1884 (Devlet 1999: 138).

Ismail Gasprinski and Jadidism

The turning point in *jadid* education system came when educator, journalist and author Ismail Gasprinski (1851-1914) announced his new education system. Later on he became famous for his slogan 'Unity in language, idea, and activity', especially among the Turkic peoples. He had received his education in a Russian military college, and had experiences of in France and the Ottoman Empire. In 1879 he tried to establish a Turkic newspaper, but couldn't get official permission but was granted permission in 1883, in the 100th anniversary of the Russian occupation of Crimea. He first tried to introduce his ideas to Russian publications and through them to the Russian administration. In his long article entitled 'Russian Muslims: Their Goals, Ideas and Observations' (*Russkoe Musulman'stwo: Mysli, zametki i nablyudenia*) which was published in the Russian newspaper *Tawrida* in 1881, he also announced his programme. He suggested in this article (a) To develop a national school and to make reforms in the education system, (b) to create charity organization for educational institutions, (c) to publish a national newspaper for all Turks in Russia in a common language, (d) to modernize the Muslim lifestyle, (e) to allow more freedom to Muslim women, and finally (f) to educate a national intellectual class. For reaching his goals he opened an *usul-i jadid* (new method) school in Bakhchesarai in 1884. For this reform school he wrote a special book, called *Khoja-i Subyan*. His success in his new method or *jadid* school certainly had an effect. And second, such a school was opened in 1887 in Khan Kirman (Kasimov). His ideas spread year after year and he had followers especially in the Volga-Ural region, which led to a serious reform movement in the educational system. In 1905 it is believed that approximately 5,000 Muslim schools were using this new method in one or the other. Not just in the Volga-Ural region, but also in Azerbaijan, Gasprinski found followers. His ideas soon spread to Central Asia.

According to Russian statistics, in 1895 the number of *maktab-madrasahs* in Kazan *gubernia* was 647 and their attendants 33,907. These numbers grew in 1911 to 132,000. In Ufa *gubernia* there were approximately 1,500 *maktab-madrasahs* and 83,000 students; in Orenburg *gubernia* 152 *madrasahs* and 226 *maktabs*, altogether 378 schools were open and 16,044 students were attending these schools (*Tarbiye ve Talim*: 189). According to official statistics on

13 September 1913 in the Volga-Ural Region, 694 native schools, 516 *maktabs* and 178 *madrasahs* were registered. But 992 *maktabs* and 35 *madrasahs* were still running in the old style.

Even though a common curriculum for all Muslim schools was accepted but to fulfil such a curriculum was not possible. First, the Muslim people of Russia didn't have a ministry of education which could enforce or control such a system. Second, all educational activities could be organized only with the help of charities given by wealthy individuals. A *jadid madrasah* consisted mainly of four types of school: *Ibtidai* (primary school) for four years; *Rushdiya* for three years; *Idadi* for three years; and *Aliya* (high school), for three years. In short, a Muslim girl or boy had to go for 12/13 years to the *madrasah* (Tatary 1967: 390). But not all *madrasahs* had all the four schools. In Kazan only the Mukhammadiya, in Orenburg the Khusayniya, and in Ufa, Aliya *madrasah* had all the four schools. Mukhammadiya was from the material and educational point of view one of the best *madrasahs*. It was attended by 500 students and had 20 professors. Not just in cities, but also in some villages like in Izhbobinsk, there were some repeated *madrasahs* (Devlet, n. 1999: 14).

The *Jadid* movement was intended to educate both boys and girls and therefore many *madrasahs* for the girls were opened, for instance, in Tetyushi (1908), Troisk (1909), Orenburg in Kazan (1913), Aitov, Khusaynov, Muteri, Abitov, Amirkhan, and Mir Haydar. In 1915 in Troisk the first Teachers College for girls was opened.

These schools were either financed by parents, wealthy persons or charitable societies. Orenburg in that respect was a leading *gubernia*. In Orenburg there were 595 mosques and in one out of two *mohallas* there was a *maktab*, and there were at least 20 charity organizations.[1]

Jadidism in the Caucasus and Central Asia

In the Caucasus, especially in South Caucasus, i.e. Azerbaijan, the reform movement started almost at the same time as in Crimea and the Volga-Ural region. Azerbaijan came under the Russian domination only after 1828. Baku, the contemporary capital of

Azerbaijan, became between 1870 and 1883 a very important industrial centre of the Russian Empire because of its oil. In 1885 the output of crude oil was 2 million tonnes per annum, in 1911 it increased to 11 million tonnes. Among Azeris there arose some reform-minded intellectuals in this period. The first among them was Abbasquli Agha Bakikhanov (1794-1847). He was a scholar, a talented poet and a historian. With his work *Gulistan-i Irem*, he awakened the historical consciousness among the Azeris. Mirza Feteli Ahundov (1812-78) was another person to have influenced Azeri literature. He was also the first to suggest to reform in the Arabic script, and in his last years he even went further as to suggest to use the Latin script. Sayyed Azim Shirvani (1835-88) was practically the first *jadidist*. He opened in his hometown in 1869 the first reformed school, where it was taught Azeri, Persian, Russian, history, geography, and mathematics. The editor of the first Turkic language newspaper *Ekinji* (Farmer) (1877-9) was Hassan Melikzade Zerdabi (1837-1907). He played a very important role in developing the *jadid* movement in Azerbaijan.

Among the Kazakhs, Chokan Velikhanov (1835-65), Ibrahim Altynsarin (1841-89) and Abay Kunanbayev (1845-1904) are accepted as the first reformists. In the development of *jadidist* ideas among the Kazakhs, the Tatars played an important role. For example, of the 509 books which were published in Kazakh until 1905, most of them were printed in Tatar printing houses (in Kazan, Orenburg, Astrakhan, Ufa, Troisk and Petersburg).

Ahmed Danish (also known as Ahmed Kalle) (1828-1904) spread the first reformist ideas among the Tajiks. His followers were Munavvar Kari (1880-1933) and Mahmud Khoja Behbudi (1874-1919). Shortly, the ideas of *jadidism* started to spread after the second half of the nineteenth century but somewhat unevenly and slowly. In some regions the response was much more positive, but still a strong opposition existed.

Jadidism in Press and Terjuman

The Volga-Ural region which was the first to come under Russian domination among the other Turkic regions, was also the first place where the ideas of reform (*jadidism*) arose. The first published

Tatar book is believed to be Sait Khalfin's *Tatar Grammar*, published in 1778. Because of the restrictions, printing activities among Tatars started later than the Russians. Between the years of 1801 and 1855 a total of 577 books were published between different Kazan printing houses. Certainly the majority of these books were religious in nature because of the Tsarist regulations.

As in the Ottoman Empire, the press activities in the Turkic world started much later than in Europe. In the case of Russian Muslims, there are some other reasons such as due to Russian oppression, who were not giving the necessary permission. The first newspaper to be published in the Ottoman Empire was *Taqvim-i Vaqayi* in 1832. An attempt to publish a bilingual Tatar-Russian newspaper *Kazanskie Izvestiya* from the Kazan University in 1808 was not successful. A second such attempt in 1834 also ended in failure.

The first Turkic newspaper could be published with the orders of the Russian Governor-General of Turkestan, General Kaufman, from Tashkent. Therefore in 1870 appeared *Turkestan Wilayetinin Gaziti*, a mixture of Chagatai and Kazakh language. Its editor was a Tatar government employee, Shahmerdan Ibrahimov till 1870. Later on, a Russian missionary and orientalist Ostromov became its editor. The newspaper appeared until 1918. But because of its official link the people of Central Asia were not interested in it.

The first non-official Turkic newspaper was *Ekinji* (Farmer) published in 1875, from Baku. The newspapers policy was not in favour of the Russian administration and when the Ottoman-Russian War broke out in 1877, the periodical was banned. But the Azeri intellectuals understood the importance of the press and tried to publish other newspapers. In 1879, in Tbilisi, Jalaleddin and Said Unsi brothers published the second Azeri newspaper, *Ziya* (Light), until 1884. In Tbilisi also appeared in the same years, *Kashkul* (Bowl) and the first Azeri journal *Ziya-i Kafkasi* (Light of Caucasus). In Tbilisi, another Azeri newspaper *Shark-i Rus* (Russian East) was published by Shahtakhtinski in 1903. Another famous Azeri intellectual Ali Merdan Topchubashev published from Baku another newspaper *Hayat* (Life) in 1904. Thus Azeris were able to publish five newspapers and one journal before the

1905 Revolution. But all were short-lived and therefore not so influential.

The Kazan Tatars were not so successful in their press activities as the Azeris before the 1905 Revolution. Altogether one journal and one newspaper could be published and both in the Russian capital of St. Petersburg, and not in Kazan or Ufa where the majority of Tatar-Bashkirs were residing. The journal *Mirat* (Mirror) was edited by the famous *kadi* (Islamic judge) Abdurreshid Ibrahimov, which started to appear in 1902 and lasted until 1908. It was a reformist and revolutionary journal. The newspaper *Nur* (Radiance) was published from St. Petersburg by Mufti Bayezidov from 1904 until 1914. The newspaper appeared for more than 10 years which can be recognized as a good performance for a Turkic newspaper in Russia.

Certainly the most important newspaper which was published in a Russian Empire was *Terjuman* (Interpreter). It was not the first newspaper in Russia, which was published in Turkish, but the first with the longest appearance record. Its publisher was the famous author, educator, politician and reformer Ismail Gasprinski. After a long struggle with the Russian authorities, he was able to get official permission for its publication. He received this permission in 1883, the hundredth anniversary of the occupation of Crimean Khanate by the Russians. Perhaps this permission was a goodwill gesture on the part of St. Petersburg. When Gasprinski was naming his newspaper he was influenced by the Turkish periodical of Shinasi Efendi's *Terjuman-i Ahwal* (Interpretation of conditions) and named it *Terjuman/Perevotchik*. In the beginning the newspaper was published in Turkic and Russian. *Terjuman* had been published between 10 April 1883 and 1918. Until 1903 the newspaper was weekly. Between 1903 and 1912 it appeared three or four times in a week, after which it became a daily. In the beginning, its circulation was only 300. After two years it had readers not only in Crimea but also in Volga-Ural region, the Caucasus, Siberia and Central Asia. The circulation at the time was 1,000 and had 300 subscribers in Crimea, 300 in the Volga-Ural region, 150 in the Caucasus, and 50 in Siberia, and 200 in Central Asia. After some years it became so popular that it had subscribers even in Cairo, India and Ottoman Turkey. According to some sources in Turkey alone 5,000 copies of *Terjuman* were sold and distributed. Gasprinski was following in his newspaper a very cautious policy, because of very strict censorship of the Russian authorities. The main goal of this newspaper was to create a 'common literature language' for all Turks (Turkic peoples). Gasprinski later started to use his famous slogan 'unity in language, idea and activity' in this paper.

Mirza Alexandar Kazem-Bek (1802-70), even as early as 1834, was defending the idea of a common language purified from all Turkic dialects. In his famous grammar book *Obshchaia Grammatika Turetsko-Tatarskogo Yazyka,* he compared Anatolian Turkish, Azeri Turkish and Tatar dialects, and showed the differences among these dialects. In other words, even he who was trying to show the common points in these dialect, couldn't escape from the reality. Also the publisher of *Ekinji* Zerdabi was all for a common Turkic language. *Terjuman's* language was much closer to Ottoman Turkish, and even today an educated Turkish intellectual can understand it. This pan-Turkic attitude was also followed in other newspapers and journals, but they were not following Gasprinski's regulations so strictly. The Russian authorities were now aware of his successes and discovering his hidden agenda. The famous missionary and orientalist, Ilminski, pointed to this fact in an official report thus:

1. Gasprinski is trying to spread the European education system without giving in to Islamic basic principles, among the Russian Muslims, and he is trying to unite Islamic ideas with European education.
2. He wants to unite the different Russian Muslims who speak in different languages and create something like a German unity.
3. With their press organs they (the Muslims) are trying to build Ottoman Turkish as a common language for all Muslims of the Turkic race.

Conclusion

The *jadid* movement in the educational system had followers not just in the Volga-Ural region but in the Caucasus, Crimea and Central Asia. In financing these *jadid maktab-madrasahs*, besides the charitable and education organisations wealthy merchants and businessmen played a great role. In Azerbaijan, Zaynalabidin Taqiev and Shemsi Asadullaev, in Volga-Ural region, Ahmad, Gani and Mahmud Hussainov, the families Yaushev, Apanay, Aktchurin and Abdulmenan, al-Haj Muhammedjan, and in Siberia al-Haj Nimatullah Karamish were the most prominent personalities who helped in the cause. The *jadid* movement, which practically started in Bakhchesarai (1884), spread to as far as Kashghar by 1906. With the financial and moral support approximately some 5,000 *jadid maktab-madrasahs* were opened. When the *kadim* (old) method was giving some restricted religious knowledge and one had to attend a school for several years just to be able to read and write, the *jadid* method was able to teach children reading and writing in 40-50 days and this they were learning apart from religion the sciences necessary for the life also (Devlet, 1999: 184).

Before the 1905 Russian Revolution there were altogether 11 periodicals and most of them short-lived. *Terjuman* among them was the most influential. But most of them were pro-reform trying to influence and to win their readers for change and reforms.[2]

In short, the *jadid* movement helped to the approximately 20 million Muslims in Russia to promote their educational level so that in 1910 they already printed more than a thousand books, published several newspapers and journals and started to struggle for their religious, cultural and even political rights in the Russian Empire.

NOTES

1. Charity organizations in Orenburg *gubernia*
   a. Orenburg Muslim Society (had a library),
   b. Troisk Muslim Charity Society (had a library called *Nedjat*),
   c. Troisk *Nashr-i Maarif* (Textbook publishing) Society,
   d. Urski Muslim Society (had a library),
   e. Chelyabinsk Library Society (was one of the richest Muslim libraries and majority of its collections were hand-written books),

f. Kargaly Muslim Society (had a library),
g. Tuez Tuebe Muslim Society,
h. Orenburg Society for Muslim Students,
i. Muslims of Orenburg Society (All these nine societies were situated in the city. Except these there were charity organizations in the villages also).

For further information see Sharaf (1913).

2.

Publication Date	Name	Publication Place	Language	Numbers
1870-1917	*Turkestan Wilayetinin geziti*	Tashkent	Chagatai-Kazakh	47 years
1875-7	*Ekinci*	Baku	Azeri	56
1879-84	*Ziya*	Tblisi	Azeri	76
1880	*Ziya-i Kafkasi*	Tblisi	Azeri	97
1883	*Kashkul*	Tblisi	Azeri	-
1883-1918	*Terjuman*	Bakhchesaray	Crimean Turkish	35 years
1888-1912	*Dala Wilayetinin geziti*	Omsk	Kazakh	24 years
1902-8	*Mir'at*	St. Petersburg	Tatar	22
1903-4	*Shark-i Rus*	Tblisi	Azeri	-
1904	*Khayat*	Baku	Azeri	-
1904-14	*Nur*	St. Petersburg	Tatar	10 years

REFERENCES

Devlet, N., 'Islam in Tataristan', *Journal of Institute of Muslim Minority Affairs*, vol. 5, no. 2 (1986).

———*Rusiya Törkilerenen Milli Köreş Tarihı (1905-1917)* (Kazan: 1998).

———*Rusya Türklerinin Milli Mücadele Tarihi (1905-1917)* [The History of the National Struggle of the Turks of Russia (1905-1917)], 2nd edn. (Ankara: 1999).

——— *İsmail Bey Gaspyraly*, 2nd edn. (Kazan: 1999).

Glazik, J., *Die Islammission der russisch-orthodoxen Kirche* (Münster: 1959).

Kanlidere, Ahmet, *Reform within Islam* (Istanbul: 1997).

Khalikov, A. Kh., *Berenche Deület* [First State] (Kazan: 1991).

Merdjani, Sh., *Mustafad el-Akhbar fi Akhvali Kazan va Bulgar* (Kazan: 1989).

Sharaf, Burkhan, 'Orenburg gubirnasynda müsülmanlar' [Muslim of Orenburg *gubernia*], *Añ*, no. 2 (Orenburg: 1913).

CHAPTER 4

Central Asian *Jadidism* and the Egyptian Islamic Reformism: Some Comparative Remarks

DILOROM AGZAMOVNA ALIMOVA

The twentieth century was a period of great changes both in the political, as well as ideological and spiritual fields in the East. Intrusion of a completely different culture, in this case the Western one sped up the processes of capitalization of economy and at the same time had a strong impact on the national consciousness and political thinking. This can be seen in connection between the traditional and the modern, in coexistence with the pre-bourgeois spiritual traditions and the secular traditions going from the West. On the other hand, the process of colonization, which came into play in the middle of the nineteenth century, stirred up the public consciousness, having strengthened the aspirations of a progressive part of the population to search for new optimum forms of struggle against the overseas intrusion. These two processes: updating of consciousness and struggle for progress are characteristic both for Egypt and for Central Asia.

If the middle of the nineteenth century was marked by the beginning of the Islamic reform cultural and ideological rise—which has come to be called *nahda* (renaissance)—the end of that century was the time of the birth of a reform movement called *jadidism*. Supporters of *nahda* aspired to synthesize elements of Western and Eastern civilizations, but they regarded the task of revival of the former power of Islamic peoples in the economic, political and cultural fields as one of paramount importance.

Supporters of both these movements tried to connect the cultural heritage of the people to the technological and cultural achievements of the West. But at the same time both of them and a few others put forward the idea of a national unity and development of a national culture for the first time in these territories. Both *nahda* and *jadidism* opened up an epoch of national awakening, an epoch of comprehension of their individuality and special place, and have became the socio-historical phenomenon answering to the needs of the emerging new bourgeoisie.

It would be incorrect to speak of the two movements as being identical, as each of them had distinct historical features and conditions. However the common idea of Islamic reformism—as religious concepts and a religious condition of the people—were an obstacle in the way of social and spiritual progress.

Protagonists of reform in Persia, Jamal Al-Din Afghani, and his Egyptian follower Shaykh Muhammad Abduh, having put forward religious reform (*al-islah i-diniy*) as the overall objective, did not stand up at all for radical restructuring and revision of basic Muslim principles, and supported revision of those elements of a traditional Islam which naturally demanded qualitative change and a different understanding as a result of public evolution.

Muslim reformers of Egypt called for clearing the dogma of distortions and the stratifications, which had been preserved for centuries, and for its updating by rejection of *bid'a*—the latest religious-dogmatic innovations. They rejected medieval scholastic understanding of Islam and the corresponding interpretation of the Koran and have followed the road of active adaptation of Muslim dogma to the requirements of engaging in a capitalist relationship.

Central Asian *jadidis* were not theologians in the full sense of the word, though their knowledge of Islam and the Koran were deep enough. They were familiar with commentaries on the Koran by Muhammad Abduh. Reformers particularly valued the problem of explanation of the place of man in the picture of the world and the role of cognition of the God and the Universe created by him.

Al-Afghani called for a revision of the dogmas constraining free inquiry, and appealed for these to be based on 'belief in man—the most noble creation of God and lord of the Earth', who is capable of learning the secrets of the being (Kirillina 1989: 130). Muhammad

Abduh shared the viewpoint of his teacher on the possibility of gaining knowledge of the objective world by use of human reasoning. The most outstanding representative of Central Asian *jadidism*, is, the great public figure, scientist and writer, Abdulrauf Fitrat, who developed this idea to appeal to the reasoning capacity of man, whose supreme purpose was to use this reason for the improvement of the world. The task of man is not simply to use the precepts ordered by the Koran, but to assume the charge of his earth and his fate. 'The man of will in the Koran is a supreme essence, he can operate the earth and the sky, transform them', writes Fitrat. If man can transform rigorous mountains on the earth, why can he not transform life, and why should he wait for a favour from rulers? He draws attention to the question, interpreting the Koran not as an appeal to show humility before destiny, but as exhorting people to make their destiny, confirming this idea by a quotation from the Book: 'Everything that man achieves, he achieves it due to desire and effort' (Fitrat 1991: 15).

Thus both the Egyptian reformers and Central Asian *jadidis* were uniform in their opinion on autonomy of the human will from divine reason. Al-Afghani opposed fatalistic judgements, appealing to Mutazilite doctrines, and excluding the absolute character of divine predetermination. Abduh analysed this problem in a pragmatic manner, emphasizing that human beings have a free will as a natural quality. In this connection he emphasized that the Koran established freedom of will (Kirillina 1989: 132).

Thus elements of fatalism were essentially limited and abstract constructions of dogmatic traditionalists about full predetermination of human destiny and measure of beyond the grave requital were criticized. In his 'Comments on the Koran' Abduh emphasized that Allah 'has granted to us reason and force, sufficient for maintenance of happiness and for distance from disasters and sufferings' (Kirillina 1989: 136).

Being based on a similar thesis, Mahmud Khoja Behbudi, the father of Central Asian jadidism, had written in an article: 'Rights are not given, they are won.' He transformed the idea of action of one person bestowing blessing on a society, into that of a group of people achieving the blessing, i.e. he asserted that nobody will give people freedom voluntarily, it should be achieved (Behbudi: 1917). Behbudi as well as many *jadidis* were against violent measures and considered it to achieve political rights within colonial administrative system through systematic parliamentary struggle.

It is well known, that both in Egypt and in Central Asia, colonial theorists tried to prove and justify expansionist aspirations of the European states, by arguing that their great mission was to bring culture and education to the backward countries. The Arabian reformists actively reacted to it. The polemical exchanges between Al-Afghani and the renowned French philosopher Ernest Renan received wide publicity. In a lecture delivered by Renan at the University of Sorbonne, he argued that Arabs are not capable of abstract thinking and scientific research. This thesis he explained by negative relation of the Muslim doctrine towards science and philosophical knowledge. Al-Afghani responded: '[d]uring the period of total ignorance Muslims found their knowledge buried in oblivion, they have [since then] revived this knowledge and have lifted science to an unprecedented height' (Kirillina 1989: 140).

The same opinions were adhered to also by the Central Asian *jadidis*. They were inclined to draw conclusions on the historical connections of Central Asia with Western Europe, focusing on modernity. Not unreasonably, they considered what exactly the Islamic culture has rescued for Europe, viz. Plato and Aristotle. And they were not simply admirers, but also new propagandists of Greek theorista to an extent. Why was Mahmud Khoja Behbudi so passionately fond of Kant's works, Fitrat—Senjoboss, Avloniy —Plato, Socrates and Aristotle—paying special attention to their views on education? One might ask, what is common in these things between the Muslim view, the basic postulate of which is obedience, and the European approach which stresses on free will? Avloniy could prove the legitimacy of these sources by Koran and on this basis to develop progressive morals for a Muslim which should be based on universal humanistic morality, and has a practical orientation and rationally serve for progress (Avloniy 1992). Fitrat's monograph *Family* based on a symbiosis of investigations of the Western sociologists and psychologists and the analysis of Islamic treatises has approximately the same orientation (Fitrat 1998: 180).

At the same time, liberating the religious views from scholasticism, they tried to return to Islam the common humanistic value, which they saw in a cultural heritage of the West. Such globalization of thinking is a characteristic feature for the most active part of the *jadid* movement. In their opinion, Central Asia being a part of the Muslim world, but representing the independent unique phenomenon in a world history, was obliged to find its worthy place in the complicated and inconsistent future which had opened up in the twentieth century.

What should determine the transition of a society into its best stage? *Jadidis* were sure that this should occur, first of all, on the basis of reforms in the field of education, through development of scientific achievements and advanced techniques, through education in spirituality for the young generation. Behbudi was rather categorical in the statement that the nations which are not incorporating advanced achievements of science and techniques will vegetate on the boondocks of world civilization. As technology was more developed in the West, attention of the *jadidis* was directed towards the West. That is why they tried to send their youth for training abroad.

In the spring and summer of 1917, *jadidis* had already actively participated in political strikes for the right to take place in the State Duma. One of the leaders of the Kadet party, N.G. Mallitsky opposed grant of any quota in elections to Muslims, calling them illiterate and ignorant people. Opposing the chauvinistic policy of Mallitsky, Behbudi spoke about the necessity of the creation of uniform structures of urban self-government for the European and Muslim parts of the city alike. 'It is wrong to consider', he said, 'that Muslims are backward and fanatical.' 'You have translated books about colonial management in India to use that system here. It would be better to publish books on how the dominant and indigenous nation will take equal elective rights and will live in conditions of equality' (*Protokoly* 1917: 29).

Central Asian *jadidis* as well as the Egyptian reformers attached huge significance to knowledge and science in the formation of a 'high-grade' outlook on personality. Behbudi considered the idea of Islamic authorities. He emphasized that without the knowledge of a history of the people, a history of the country, and a history of Islam, the existence of neither a simple Muslim nor a statesman, neither a servant of Islam nor a scientist is possible. History, according to his opinion, explains everything: the reasons for the blossoming and decline of the state; the condition of belief of people; degradations of Islam; a distortion of the initial foundations of Islam, etc. (Behbudi 1914: 502-5). Also, the views of protagonists of both the movements towards state system are similar. Abduh considered that constitutional management can be achieved by peaceful arrangements with the government. Such a position is characteristic of Bukhara *jadidis* of the first generation who wanted to keep the Amir's authority and to devise a constitutional monarchy.

They maintained that it was necessary to prepare the population for change in the form of government in a state and believed the extensive training was required to help the people and the authorities alike to comprehend the necessity of the establishment of parliamentary democracy.

Many people criticized Abduh for using the help of foreigners in carrying out social and religious reforms in the country. On that he answered: 'Sacred Koran, time and experience of our ancestors advise us and allow us to use non-believers and non-Muslims for the benefit of Muslims (Kirillina 1989: 154). This attitude was determined by sober reflections concerning arrangement of political forces in the country.

Such position was characteristic also for the Central Asian *jadid* movement, which in the beginning had mainly an educational character within the framework of activities allowed by the Russian administration. Nevertheless, the intellectual explosion in Central Asia, having a centuries-old genesis and caused by struggle against the Russian colonization, especially by the revolt of 1916, had developed by 1917 into a sociopolitical outburst. By then, it became clear that the development of culture and education is impossible without social and political perfection, which in turn, was impossible to attain within the colonial framework. Efforts to achieve progress are destined for success only when the state is interested in it. *Jadidis* understood the situation and for this reason, knowing a real situation in which independence was not possible, they tried to establish independent national statehood—*Turkistan Muhtoriati*—within the framework of the Russian Federation. Certainly, it was state formation within a state, but with precise differentiations of the competence of Central Asian republic and the Russian federal centre, the powers of which were reduced to a minimum. This formation denoted the perception of impossibility of a full separation at that juncture and at the same time it was also a claim for political independence. If it was difficult to imagine Bolsheviks being reconciled to this phenomenon, national democrats would go further. Long before these events Ahmad Danish wrote at the end of the nineteenth century: 'Now the way of enmity and conflicts with Russia is closed, now it is necessary to establish the order combining Bukharian and Russian (elements). And then, if it is required, there will be an open collision' (Danish: 1987). Behbudi at the congress of Executive Committees of the Central Asia, in April 1917, asserting equality in rights in the participation of indigenous population in elective bodies, spoke: 'If Russians will not agree with this, Muslims should be separated with formation of the conciliatory commission on the general questions' (*Protokoly* 1917: 29). Thus, Behbudi in the direct image hinted that in an unprofitable allocation of political forces in Turkistan, local progressive people will make efforts for the organization of the national statehood.

At the same time, he considered that a condition for this purpose is association of all nations and peoples living in the territory of Turkistan. He wrote: 'We want, using the participation of Russians, Jews and others to found such a Turkistani government and the parliament in which Muslims could live according to the laws and religion. The laws thus created should protect interests of all: Jews, Christians and Muslims' (*Ulug Turkiston*: 1917).

Such tolerance of *jadidis* had certainly very deep roots, much before the historical coexistence of the most ancient religions in Central Asia before the occurrence of Islam. Speaking about association of Muslims, as different from the Egyptian reformers, *jadidis* never thought about the creation of a monolithic state. Yet, the *jadidis* were criticized for adopting a secular position.

Such criticism came from a part of the organisation 'Council of Ulema' and by the more conservative part of the population which was under the influence of the clergy. There is a question: if the *jadidis* accepted the Western samples of culture, why did they not categorically accept Marxism? They approached Western philosophical ideas selectively, using only those that can coexist within the boundaries of local religious perceptions. In Behbudi's positivism lay the main line of philosophy of the *jadid* movement.

For them, religion was not a political instrument; it was a means of clarification from ignorance. They were honest in their religious feelings. But despite their religiousness they represented the future state system of Central Asia as secular, based on democratic laws and parliamentarism. Why did the population support their attempt at construction of a secular state with national features? It is known, that during three months of existence of *Turkiston Mukhtoriati*, mass meetings passed resolutions in its support in all regions. The reason, in my opinion, is that here the ground was prepared by Islamic legal theory about the state evolving over many centuries and going beyond religious sphere of application. The legal philosophy of the Orient put forward the idea of sovereignty of rulers much earlier than in Europe. As early as twelfth-fifteenth centuries, al-Farabi and Ibn Khaldun had put forward such an argument, and Alisher Navoi put forward the idea of electivity of the supreme government. More specifically, like al-Farabi and Ibn Sina before him, Ahmad Danish at the end of the nineteenth century saw principles of statehood in social association of people, although he derived his views from the progressive *jadid* movement enriched by its knowledge about the European political philosophy (Danish: 1987).

Al-Afghani considered the major strategic task to be the formation of an association of Muslims under the aegis of the pious caliph, capable of resisting colonial aspirations of Europe. 'The Muslim countries' projects he addressed to Egyptian Khadiv Ismail, to Iranian Shah Naser al-Din Shah, and to the Turkish Sultan Abdulhamid II.

Dissimilarity of both reformatory movements, in our opinion, consists in that Egyptians did not have the problem of heterogeneity of the population. Central Asia was occupied from time immemorial by representatives of various Iranian, Macedonian and Turkic ethnicities. Probably this can explain going out of the narrow national frameworks, the aspiration to unite all nations and nationalities in Central Asia and to get rid of internal disagreements and contradictions. Behbudi wrote in this occasion:

> . . . It is necessary for us to renounce first of all an opposition to Kadimists and Jadids and to achieve finding the uniform union. We want that Muslims of Turkistan in unity with local Russians, Jews and all representatives of the nations living here, . . . , that the laws focused for the blessing of all Jews living in Turkistan, Christians, Muslims have been made. If we shall be united, there will be progress for religion, the nation, fatherland. And today we, Muslims are dependent on the Russians. We are a colony, owing to our disagreements.
> (Behbudi: 1917)

Positions of both directions of reformatory movement and in questions of education, the relation to position of women, necessities of emancipation distinguished by comprehension, but rather constrained methods which do not contradict Muslim dogma, were similar.

Representatives of both movements realized the necessity of careful work with the native language that was dictated by the concept of national revival, but they realized also the importance of mastering the European languages. As Abduh said: 'he who does not know even one European language, can never become a scientist in our century' (Kirillina 1989: 170). Behbudi's credo was 'for us four languages are necessary, and not one' (Behbudi: 1913). To be expert in laws and in a modern life, in his opinion it was necessary to know Turkish, Persian, and some European languages.

Thus comparing the two reformatory movements, so remote from each other geographically, but incorporated within the richest Islamic heritage, we can draw conclusions on their spiritual generality and at the same time the bright individuality determined by national features.

It is impossible to agree with the Soviet treatment of these movements as being limited to extremely narrow frameworks, suggesting conservative credentials. Certainly, both the Egyptian reformers and Central Asian *jadids* were not free from mistakes, however in certain moral, spiritual, and political conditions they operated according to historical circumstances.

REFERENCES

Avloniy, A., *Turkiy guliston yohud axloq* (Tashkent, 1992).

Behbudi, M., 'Bayoni hakikat', *Ulug Tirkiston*, 12 June 1917.

———'Bir til emas, tort til kerak', *Oina*, no. 1, 30 August 1913.

——— 'Kasb olinur, berilmas', *Hurriyat*, no. 22, 13 July 1917.

——— 'Tarih va jugrofia', *Oyna*, no. 29, 1914.

Danish, Ahmad, *Risalah Tarikh Amiron Mangyt* (Rudaki Insitute of Oriental Studies, 1987).

Fitrat, A., 'Hind sayehining hissasi', *Shark yulduzi*, no. 8, 1991.

——— *Oila eki boshkarish tartiblari. Baku 1915*, Tashkent, 1998.

Kirillina, S.A., *Islam v obshestvennoi zhizni Egipta*, 1989.

Protokoly s'ezda delegatov Ispolnitelnyh komitetov Turkestanskogo kraya, 9-16, Tashkent, April 1917.

Ulug Turkiston, 12 June 1917.

CHAPTER 5

'Young India: A Bengal Eclogue', or Meat-eating, Race, and Reform in a Colonial Poem

ROSINKA CHAUDHURI

This essay uses a poem written by an Englishman, Henry Meredith Parker, in early nineteenth-century Calcutta, 'Young India: A Bengal Eclogue', to examine the contexts of reform, revision, and writing in Bengal in the 1820s and the 1830s. The reform movement known as 'Young Bengal' has been strangely bypassed in post-colonial narratives; yet this was a historical and epistemological moment that defined the shape of modern India. Radical and yet imitative, the movement incorporated paradoxes that continue to inhabit Indian public life. Certainly its main impulses found a continuum in the nationalist movement; Gandhi, typically, subverted one of its principles of heresy, the consumption of beef in order to overthrow the hefty English, into a mantra of vegetarianism. Its imitative element was instantly material for satire; Bengalis themselves lampooned the follies of Young Bengal mercilessly in various media, as did Parker in his poem. Also implicated in the politics of meat-eating in the nineteenth century was the construction of the manly Englishman in contrast to the Indian male whose effeminacy was invariably linked to his education, as demonstrated in many of Kipling's works. The essay therefore also explores the deterioration in race relations from the time of one Anglo-Indian poet, Henry Meredith Parker, to another, Rudyard Kipling, showing how an acquired intimacy with the colonized gave way to a deliberate new imperialism permeated with a prejudice and ignorance that served to exclude Europeans from many areas of Indian life.

Kings, Priests, and Laws, and Creeds, are but the tools
Which cunning knaves employ to govern fools;
Down with Kings, Laws and Creeds then, and in chief
With any creed prohibiting roast beef.

'Young India: A Bengal Eclogue'
(Henry Meredith Parker 1851: 225)

A doggerel of the Gujarati poet Narmad was in vogue amongst us schoolboys, as follows:

'Behold the mighty Englishman
He rules the Indian small,
Because being a meat-eater
He is five cubits tall.'
All this had its due effect on me. I was beaten. It began to grow on me that meat-eating was good,
that it would make me strong and daring, and that, if the whole country took to meat-eating,
the English could be overcome.

(Gandhi 1982: 35)

Nationalist as well as post-colonial studies of colonial history, in a rare show of unity, have always emphasized the epistemic moment when the government of India, under William Bentinck, implemented an English education for Indians in 1835. Macaulay's infamous minute on education, which was instrumental in getting Bentinck's bill passed, argued for 'a class of persons, Indian in blood and colour, but English in taste, in opinions, in morals, and in intellect'.[1] Macaulay's motives might have been influenced by commercial considerations ('to trade with civilised men is infinitely more profitable than to govern savages' (Speech of 10 July 1833), but Indians themselves had been negotiating for English education in India long before him. Indians, both radical (Rammohun Roy) and conservative (Radhakanta Deb, Ramkamal Sen), first led the movement towards English education through the establishment of the Hindu College in 1817, wishing 'to be informed of everything that the English gentlemen learnt, and they would take that which they found good and liked best'.[2] Macaulay's minute on education had borrowed some key points from Roy, but Roy was working towards his own independent agenda—fashioning a new ideology for the advancement of his countrymen, 'at least for the sake of their political advantage and social comfort' (Biswas 1992: 400-1). Almost a decade before Macaulay, Rammohun Roy had pointed out in 1823 that if 'the improvement of the native population is the object of the Government, it will consequently promote a more liberal and enlightened system of instruction, embracing Mathematics, Natural Philosophy, Chemistry, Anatomy, with other useful sciences' (Ghosh 1885: 465).

It was only after 1835 that schemes for the moral and political improvement of Indians flowed ardently from Anglo-Indian[3] policy-makers such as Macaulay and his brother-in-law Charles Trevelyan, a member of the Secretariat at Calcutta under William Bentinck. Among Indians, however, succeeding the lone crusader Rammohun, the drive for reform, based on the redemptive idea of a mission to reform India, had become the domain of an entire class since at least 1826, when Derozio joined the Hindu College. This reform movement, downplayed in post-colonial perspectives, was constituted, paradoxically, of radical dimensions co-existing with forms of imitation and parody, cutting across assumptions about colonial societies. This article uses a little-known poem, 'Young India: A Bengal Eclogue', that is itself situated in the confluence of margin and centre by virtue of having been written by an Englishman in colonial Calcutta about young Bengalis, to examine that context of reform and revision initiated in Bengal from 1827 to the 1830s by a section of Indians. I show here how elements of that original impulse of reform found a response in Gandhi and the nationalist movement, except that while Nehru continued to inhabit that climate of Western liberalism, Gandhi, typically, shifted the emphasis, intuitively voicing the taste of the general Indian public.

'A New Race of Men in the East'

Writing from Calcutta in the early nineteenth century, eminent Anglo-Indian poet Henry Meredith Parker (1796-1868), in his poem, 'Young India: A Bengal Eclogue', lampooned a notorious as well as celebrated chapter of nationalist Indian history: 'Young Bengal'. That nomenclature[4] was given to a group of students at the

Hindu College in the late 1820s and early 1830s, radicals who based their challenge to Hindu orthodoxy on the tenets of progressive Western thought. They were also known as 'Derozians' after their teacher Henry Derozio, one contemporary even referring to them as 'Young Calcutta' (Mittra 1877: 28). Derozio's students signified the emergence of a class, composed almost entirely of those who had received an organized public instruction in the English language, that could be defined for the first time as an intelligentsia in the Western sense of the term. The ardour of Young Bengal for the ideological freedoms preached through an English education sometimes took on an adolescent character, but nevertheless acquired a striking seriousness in the Calcutta society of the 1830s. The youth of this generation led hitherto unthinkable attacks on the conventions of traditional Hinduism; examples include Rasik Krishna Mullick's open denial of the sanctity of the Ganges and Ramgopal Ghose's refusal to undergo the ritual of penance (Gupta 1958: 19). K.M. Banerji, one of the earliest converts to Christianity among the members of Young Bengal, had declared in 1830 that Pope and Dryden were to be held in higher esteem than the Hindu *Shastras* (Sen 1932: 141-2) Peary Chand Mittra comments on these young men's penchant for 'ridiculing the Hindu religion', citing instances when, 'they were required to utter *mantras* or prayers, [but instead] repeated lines from the *Iliad*. There were some who flung [*sic*] the Brahminical thread instead of putting it on' (Mittra 1877: 16). One of the newspapers of the period memorably accused the youth of this generation of 'cutting their way through ham and beef and wading to liberalism through tumblers of beer' (Sen 1932: xxviii).

Parker's title for his poem is 'Young India' rather than 'Young Bengal' consequently, the group of people under discussion is given a larger significance as the emerging identity of modern India. Subverting the expectations that the latter half of its title, 'A Bengal Eclogue', creates of a pastoral dialogue, the poem consists instead of a dialogue between two Bengali students of the 'Anglo-Indian College' (Hindu College) in Calcutta.[5] These two urban youths, 'with Muslin robes and frizzled hair', are shown strolling at the base of Ochterlony's column in Calcutta at twilight. They are dressed contrastingly, one traditionally and effeminately, in *pyjamas* and 'spangled slipper', with 'many a yard' of thread round his neck (referring to the sacred thread of the Brahmin), and the other, following Western, almost military, masculinity, in 'Irish linen shorts', 'polish'd jockey boot[s]', 'a watch', 'a bunch of seals' and 'guard' (Parker 1851: 223). The latter is called 'Hurry Mohun Bhose' (Hari Mohan Bose) and the former 'Sam Chund' (Shyam Chand). Parker does not make a mistake in this minor detail concerning the names; the traditionalist who wears the sacred thread, the reluctant friend, is the representative of Brahmin orthodoxy while the passionate liberal has a common Kayastha surname, Bose, suggestive of an aspiring, anglicized background.

Hurry Mohun begins his speech on a high note, invoking the virtues of liberty. He mentions France first, followed by 'shades of all the Bruti', Cobden and William Tell, 'Freedom's sworn children each, from wig to shoe tye' (Parker 1851: 224-5). After Sam Chund asks him to get to the point, he does so:

> Kings, Priests, and Laws, and Creeds, are but the tools
> Which cunning knaves employ to govern fools,
> Down with Kings, Laws and Creeds then, and in chief
> With any creed prohibiting roast beef.

Roast beef, to much comical effect, is at the centre of the young men's thoughts in this poem. Outside of it, however, it was an immensely serious issue in Indian society, one that provoked hysterical responses from orthodox Hindus. It was also an issue inextricably linked to the free-thinking Young Bengal, who were primarily concerned with challenging the traditional strictures of Hinduism, one of which forbade the consumption of beef. The activities of Derozio's Academic Association correspond with Parker's observation of the revolutionary sentiments expressed in the poem—'Down with Kings, Laws and Creeds . . .':

> Free-will, fore-ordination, fate, faith, the sacredness of truth, the high duty of cultivating virtue, and the meanness of vice, the nobility of patriotism, the attributes of God, and the argument for and against the existence of the deity as these have been set forth by Hume on the one side, and Reid, Dugald Stewart and Brown on the other, the hollowness of idolatry and the shams of priesthood were subjects which stirred to their very depths the young,

fearless, hopeful hearts of the leading Hindoo youths of Calcutta. (Edwards 1884: 32)

Alexander Duff wrote disapprovingly that 'Their great authorities . . . were Hume's Essays and Paine's *Age of Reason*. With copies of the latter, in particular, they were abundantly supplied . . . ' (Duff: 1839, 616). This revolt against religious superstition, then, was not only the outcome of colonial contact with British liberalism, as is often presumed in post-colonial studies, but also directly linked to Tom Paine's philosophy of individual rights. Paine was read avidly by students of the Hindu College at that time; Duff despaired of the craven commercial considerations that brought Paine's book to Calcutta. 'It was some wretched bookseller in America, who, —basely taking advantage of the reported infidel leanings of a new race of men in the East, and apparently regarding no God but his silver dollars,—dispatched to Calcutta a cargo of that most malignant and pestiferous of all anti-Christian publications.

From one ship a thousand copies were landed, and at first sold at the cheap rate of one rupee per copy; but such was the demand, that the price soon rose, and after a few months, it was actually quintupled. Besides the separate copies of the *Age of Reason*, there was also a cheap American edition, in one thick volume, containing all of Paine's works, including the *Rights of Man*, and other minor pieces, political and theological.

The phenomenal response to this cargo among Calcutta's 'new race of men' gives an indication of the background which made possible Parker's depiction of Hurry Mohun's character and charter of demands.

'Freedom and Beef Steaks'

Hurry Mohun, continuing his tirade, turns to education, progress, and the 'Rail Roads, which exstatic joy / Inspired in Maha Raj Ram Mohun Roy!' (Parker 1851: 225). Rammohun Roy's contribution to the discourse of reform that emerged in early nineteenth-century Bengal was seminal. These included the establishment of a monotheist Hindu reform church, a vigorous campaign for legislation against *sati*, and also, as we have seen, an active advocacy of Western education for Indians. Here he is nonsensically linked to the railway (he died in 1833, while the railway came to India in 1853), that other great symbol of progressiveness in colonial India. The reference to Roy is actually important in the context of the ideal mentioned alongside roast beef, 'Freedom'—'Your mind shall . . . soar at once to Freedom and Beef Steaks' (Parker 1851: 225)—which, here, implies not so much freedom from British rule, but freedom from the backwardness of Indian society.

The poem's protagonist, unsurprisingly in such a context, was most probably based on a real person; one among Derozio's inner circle of students was Radhanath Sikdar, immortalized in history as 'a mathematician and free-thinker with a somewhat satirical faith in the efficacy of beef as a factor in national development' (Dover 1936: 110-11). Peary Chand Mittra also catalogues Sikdar's obsession, observing, 'Radha Nauth Sickdar [*sic*] had an ardent desire to benefit his country. His hobby was beef, as he maintained that beefeaters were never bullied, and that the right way to improve the Bengalees was to think first of the *physique* or perhaps *physique* and *morale* simultaneously' (Mittra 1877: 32). Sikdar's views were sufficiently infamous for it to be almost certain that Parker would have heard about them, and in this poem, he is quick to pick up on the potential for comedy in the situation, continuing Hurry Mohun's tirade with sentiments that Sikdar would no doubt have approved of:

Roast beef! to what do these pale English owe,
(Or rather, yellow English,) that the blow
Of British arms is strong, their heads are thick,
And, therefore, fitted for the frequent lick? (Parker 1851: 225)

In a different but related context, a pamphlet written in 1875 by Henry Woodrow, the Director of Public Instruction in Bengal, incorporates a typical discussion on the character of the Bengali race. Concluding that Bengalis cannot compete with the sturdier races of the North-Western Provinces, 'but they are vastly superior to them in brains', Woodrow recommends that, in the Civil Service colleges, those subjects be taught in which the Bengali was least efficient; that is, 'attention was [to be] given to gymnastics, by which physical strength might be developed' (Woodrow 1875: 326-7). In 1871-2, Sir George Campbell had implemented a scheme where candidates for appointments with a salary of over Rs. 100 a month had to show that they could ride at least twelve miles at a rapid pace, and those applying for lesser jobs show that they would 'be able to walk twelve miles within three hours and a half without difficulty or prostration.' Such tests, Campbell thought, were good and necessary, and he believed he could not have done a greater kindness to the natives of Bengal than by holding out to them such standards, 'by which they may gradually fit themselves to emulate Europeans' (Woodrow 1875: 329).

Parker's poem might have been a repository of like-minded prejudices; certainly, Parker reveals similar race-thinking elsewhere in comparing Hindu and Muslim characteristics:

> The Moosulmann, with his brief, bald "Ullah il Ullah; Mahommed Rusool e Ullah" is a buffalo; fierce, thick-skinned, hard, dogged; against whom the arrows of truth are launched in vain. The Hindoo is a jackal; crafty, wily, subtle, shifty, evasive; whose controversial teeth are more sharp than most of us dream, and whose skin hangs so loosely on him that you cannot grasp it without immense difficulty. (Parker 1858: 18)

Again, while narrating an instance of Bengali Muslims believing in Hindu caste, Parker recalls how, upon being upbraided for clinging to Hindu prejudices, 'the unorthodox reprobates stood pale—with the green paleness of frightened Bengallys' (Parker 1858: 21).

The European perception of Hindus, specifically Bengalis, as a passive and effeminate people goes back to the beginnings of colonial rule. In *Colonial Masculinity*, Mrinalini Sinha traces, in one instance, the course of this prejudice from Richard Orme in the 1770s and Bishop Heber in the 1820s, through Evangelical and Utilitarian contributors such as Charles Grant and James Mill, to the most eloquent passages on the subject in Macaulay's essay on Clive. Her thesis on 'the manly Englishman' and the 'effeminate Bengali *babu*' in the late nineteenth-century studies the construct of colonial masculinity in a densely historicized context, showing how effeminacy was an attribute associated specifically with Western-educated Indians, a large majority of whom were

Bengali Hindus. The term *babu* came to be applied to politically discontented Indians in general. Sinha quotes from the native-owned *Amrita Bazaar Patrika*: 'if any one of the dumb millions gets his tongue, he becomes a *babu* at once and then it is only a *babu* who speaks' (Sinha 1995: 15-16).

The importance of diet, allied to the construction of masculinity, remained an important feature of the Indian nationalist agenda to reform the old, and model a new, strong, and independent country. Along with the removal of social evils such as *sati*, child marriage and caste, Indian reformers wished to institute, for the progress of society, a Western education, and also a Western diet. It was not until Gandhi went on to turn the tables in favour of vegetarianism that a nationalist consensus was articulated against the liberal concept that meat-eating was essential for reform in India. Gandhi wrote substantially on nutrition and diet, advocating vegetarianism in theories that were as involved and elaborate as his political and social writings—indeed, for him the two were inseparable. Inverting the argument put forward by Radha Nath Sickdar, he advocated the correct vegetarian diet to his followers to enable them to free India from its servitude to beef-eating Englishmen. Gandhi describes the argument of his meat-eating friend in his autobiography:

> We are a weak people because we do not eat meat. The English are able to rule over us, because they are meat-eaters. You know how hardy I am, and how great a runner too. It is because I am a meat-eater. Meat-eaters do not have boils or tumours, and even if they sometimes happen to have any, these heal quickly. Our teachers and other distinguished people who eat meat are no fools. They know its virtues. You should do like-wise. . . . (Gandhi 1982: 34)

The perception of the superior strength and physique of the master-race in the fictional Hurry Mohun to Gandhi's friend, lay also in the ascendance of what Robert Young calls 'racialism—that is, theories of race offered as a form of scientific knowledge about mankind', whose explicit theorization began 'in the late eighteenth century, [and] were increasingly scientificized in the nineteenth' (Young 1995: 91-2). The idea of the superiority of the white race, and, in many instances, specifically, of English gentlemen (over middle class and Irish competitionwallahs in the Indian Civil Service, for example), began increasingly to appear in Anglo-Indian papers and to be applied in public commissions and governmental decisions in India, quickly permeating through to the popular imagination. The desire for strength, for reform, and for an independent India led Gandhi, in the 1880s, to eat meat against all the cherished practices of his Vaishnava community and family, because 'my mind was bent on the "reform" . . . I wished to be strong and daring and wanted my countrymen also to be such, so that we might defeat the English and make India free. . . . The frenzy of the "reform" blinded me' (Gandhi 1982: 35).

That frenzy of reform, sweeping through a town in Gujarat at the end of the century, began, in fact, in the classrooms of the Hindu College and in the initiatives of Young Bengal. A modern historian comments on how Derozio's Academic Association launched a bold, uncompromising attack on Hinduism, denouncing it as 'vile and corrupt. . . . As time passed . . . more frequent was the cry, down with orthodoxy; down with tradition.' An incident in 1831 brought matters to a fever pitch. A student of Hindu College threw roast beef into a neighbouring Brahmin's house, shouting to the horrified inmates, 'Beef ! Beef !' (Bhattacharya 1980: 9).

1831 was also the year in which Derozio died, two years after these extreme attitudes had so alarmed the managing committee of Hindus at the College that he had been forced to submit his resignation.[6]

Literature dominated the age, as did also Western philosophy, religion, history and science, all bracketed under the aegis of 'an English education'. The agency of the Hindu College, alias the Anglo-Indian College, in effecting the changing priorities of the time is mentioned in Parker's poem when, reacting to Sam Chund's objections to eating beef—'What would the goddess say? and what mamma? / Srii might chastise me, so might my papa. / I cannot go your lengths, indeed I can't, / Besides next week's the Shrad for my dead aunt.'— Hurry Mohun is indignation itself:

Is this alas! the fruit of all the knowledge
We gathered at the Anglo-Indian College?
Was it for *this* we learned the world was round,

That twenty shillings sterling make a pound;
That spinning jennies, Sam, were not young ladies,
And what a science is, and what a trade is?
Was it for *this* my essay, proved, (signed JUSTUS),
That Dryden wrote his Virgil for Augustus?
Was it for this we thought Crabbe's Penseroso
And Sampson Agonisthes, rather so so;
Scott's Comus dull, but Milton's song divine
Of Johnny Gilpin, very, very, fine? (Parker 1851: 227)

The high seriousness of 'fruit of . . . knowledge', with its resonance of the Old Testament and Milton, rhymed with, in the next line, 'Anglo-Indian College', turns the question posed into a parody and joke. Published in 1851, Parker's lines also parody the cadences of Wordsworth's *Prelude*, brought out posthumously the year before ('Was it for this/That one, the fairest of all rivers, loved/ To blend his murmurs with my nurse's song. . . . For this didst thou, O Derwent! winding among grassy holms.').[7]

Parker, almost in Edward Lear style, rubbishes the knowledge of English literature acquired by these young Indians, according to whom, nonsensically, Dryden writes his Virgil for Augustus; *Comus* is attributed to Scott rather than Milton and called dull; while Milton is apparently admired, and *Samson Agonistes* is spelt wrongly. The signature attributed to the essay-writer, JUSTUS, is very funny, picking up as it does one of the fashions of the time, Derozio himself having contributed to the *India Gazette* under the pseudonym 'Juvenis'. The poem ends with a concession on the part of Sam Chund, who agrees, finally, to eat some veal. Hurry Mohun is satisfied, as everything cannot be expected to be achieved all together, and the 'expectant world' watches while Sam ponders on his 'course of cutlet', and waits for the day when his mind shall soar, finally, to 'Freedom and Beef Steaks' (Parker 1851: 228).

Satirizing the Babu

Parker's ridicule for the literariness of these anglicized students has something in common with many critiques of Young Bengal by Bengalis themselves, where these intellectuals were criticized for being 'denationalized' and 'hyper-Westernized' while denying the validity of their entire cultural heritage.[8] An example of this attitude may be found in the sentimental eloquence of literary historian Dinesh Chandra Sen, who accused these Westernized young men of forgetting their own indigenous literature:

> Young Bengal, as the new generation of the Bengalis were then called, became thoroughly anglicized in spirit. They exulted in Shakespeare's dramas and Milton's poetry; they read Schiller's *Robbers* and Goethe's *Faust*; they could name all the English dramatists of the Elizabethan age—Marlow, Philip Massinger, Ford, John Webster, Ben Johnson and Shirley and reproduce from memory lines from still earlier dramatists and from Holinshed's chronicles which Shakespeare had improved on, in many a noble line. They grew mad after Shelley's *Epipsychidion*, Keat's [*sic*] *Hyperion* and even after Chatterton's *Death of Charles Bodwin*. Poor Chandi Das, poor Vidyapati and Kavi Kankana! the tears of your departed spirit fell on the big towns of Bengal which lay under the charm of European influence, — mixed with nocturnal dews and unheeded by Young Bengal. (Sen 1911: 883)

In all fairness, it must be mentioned that Sen's monumental work, which had been published originally in Bengali in 1896, had institutionalized much of the medieval Bengali literature presented in it for the first time. 'We did not know that there was such a vast entity as early Bengali literature', wrote Rabindranath Tagore after the second edition appeared in 1898 (Ghosh 1990: 225). The rich literary heritage of Bengal presented by Sen would not have been available to the members of Young Bengal as an established canon at a time when Bengali was still largely an oral and non-literary language.

Bengalis satirized the effete *babus* of their day variously through lampoons, songs, journalism, literature and even popular paintings such as the Kalighat *pat*. As early as 1823, the Bengali writer Bhavanicharan Bandopadhyay (1787-1848) had ridiculed the contemporary *babu* for his absence of roots in Indian traditional culture. His opinion, in *Kalikata Kamalalay (Calcutta, Home of Kamala [Goddess of Wealth])*, was that this new breed of men was not truly great, but composed of those that had simply grown rich by canvassing, commissioning, cheating and pimping. Bhavanicharan also pilloried extravagant upstart *babu* culture in social sketches such as *Nababababubilas* (*Enjoyments of the New*

Babu, 1825) and *Nababibibilas* (*Enjoyments of the New Woman*, 1831). Peary Chand Mittra (1814-83), the famous Derozian, gave a scathing account of decadent *babus* in his novel, *Alaler Ghare Dulal* (*The Rich Man's Spoilt Child*, 1858), while Kaliprasanna Singha's (1840-70), *Hutom Penchar Naksha* (*The Night Owl's Sketch*, 1862) was a lively satire of *Babu* culture. Two plays on similar themes, Michael Madhusudan Dutt's (1824-73) *Ekei ki Baley Sabhyata?* (*Is This Civilisation?* 1860) and Dinabandhu Mitra's (1829-74) *Sadhabar Ekadashi* (*The Wife's Widow-Fast*, 1866) are so popular that they are staged even today.

It was, however, Kaliprasanna Singha's running commentary on the contemporary culture of his time that was the most colloquial and pungent. He describes the current breed of *babus* in his typically trenchant elliptical style:

> These days the city's English-style babus belong to two factions, the first group, 'Cow dung busts of superior model sahibs'; the second 'Vile reflections of the foreigner'. All those who belong to the first lot follow the English fashion, they assemble around tables and chairs, tea in tea cups, cheroots, water in jugs, brandy in decanters, and cork covers for glasses, covers of red cotton cloth—the *Harkara*, *Englishman*, and the *Phoenix* lie before them, Politics and *Best News of the Day* are the subjects of perpetual argument. They eat on tables, defecate in commodes and wipe their bums with paper. They are ornamented with the various virtues of compassion, pity, benevolence, meekness; only are always prone to disease, drunkenness and being slaves to their wives,—enthusiasm, unity, desire for progress having been entirely exiled from their hearts. These are the old class.
>
> In the second—Bagambar Mitra etc.—are those more dreadful than snakes, more fierce than tigers; in other words these are a type of terrible animal. These people, in the manner of thieves who touch alcohol to their lips in order to impersonate drunks when they go out to steal, pretend to care for the welfare of their country only in their own selfish interest. 'How to become rich themselves' 'how to keep everybody else under their thumb', these are their constant efforts—riding piggyback on others' labours while preening their own whiskers, this is their policy. Charity is unknown amongst them—they never have more than four annas to donate. (Nag 1991: 46-7)

Bagambar Mitra is an allusion to Digambar Mitra (1817-97), a student of Hare School and Hindu College, and one of the most prominent of Derozio's students (Nag 1991: 53). The luxury and corruption of old-style *babus* is denigrated, but the reforming instincts of self-styled saviours of society among the newer, more radical Derozians is considered even more dangerous. This type of radical young man, satirized by Parker in 'Young India', was also the concern of Bengal's leading writer in the latter half of the century, Bankim Chandra Chatterjee (1838-94). In his 'Confessions of a "Young Bengal"' Bankim's *Babu* declares, 'We have cast away caste. We have outlived the absurdity of a social classification based upon the accident of birth. But we are not such ultra-radicals as to adopt for our catchword the impracticable formula of 'Equality and Fraternity'(Chatterjee 1969: 139; my translation).[9]

Parker, thus, shares an attitude with these Bengali writers: the students in 'Young India' too wish to cast away caste but are 'not such ultra-radicals' as to risk being excommunicated in a hurry (at the end of the poem they agree, in theory, to eat veal but are not shown actually doing so). Such a writer belongs to the middle ground between the West's Orientalism and the world of the colonized, for, although Parker is observant about and sensitive to the situation of the colonized, he cannot share their predicament. Belonging to the middle-classes himself (he was said to have been a violinist at Covent Garden before the influence of Lord Moira enabled him to enter the Service), and writing poetry about the middle-class East from Calcutta, he occupies the margins of both the English literary canon (Byron, Moore, Southey) as well as of the English establishment in India.[10] Here we find that, in the history of Western writings about the East, some works produced by the intelligentsia of the colonizers, to paraphrase Aijaz Ahmed, disrupt 'the very Western canonicity which, Said complains, has always silenced the Orient' (Ahmed 1994: 174). British officials like Parker interacted with a section of Indians to build *together* a discourse that qualifies the Orientalist discourse which Said and others have interpreted as a purely Western intellectual construct.

Race Relations: Parker, Derozio, Kipling

Parker's intimacy with Derozio in Calcutta in the late 1820s resulted in the choice of Derozio's students as the protagonists of his poem. That choice of subject was very unusual for the time.

Parker wrote in an age of intense cultural engagement with the Orient, whose mood was best exploited by Byron, who, in May 1813, wrote to the Irish poet Thomas Moore, urging him to join the bandwagon of 'oriental' poetry: 'Stick to the East . . . it [is] the only poetical policy. . . . The little I have done in that way is merely a "voice in the wilderness" for you; and, if it has had any success, that also will prove that the public are orientalizing, and pave the path for you.'[11] In *Bole Ponjis*, Parker published his own literary manifesto against exactly such an 'orientalizing' of tastes, warning his reader against wandering 'into realms of Orientalism, such as mine are, under an impression that she or he would there be amidst regions resembling, however faintly, those made glorious and gorgeous by Lord Byron and Thomas Moore. . . .'[12] On the contrary, displaying a determination to work against the dominant Western demand for certain chosen ideas and images of the East, his poems, Parker insists, are 'of the East Easty; but of no such East as the reader has, probably, been familiar with. No "Gardens of *gul* in her bloom."[13] No lands "Where all but the spirit of man is divine," — but the simple prosaic East of this every day world . . .' (Parker 1851: 139).[14]

That 'simple prosaic East of this every day world', for Parker, was where he spent his entire working life, arriving in Calcutta at the age of seventeen or eighteen, in 1815 or 1816, and leaving in 1842 after a career in the Bengal Civil Service and a literary career that began in the columns of the *Calcutta Journal* (Calcutta: 1818-24). Except for a few sketchy notices in various biographical dictionaries, no comprehensive source of information exists on this Calcutta man of letters. While these invariably tell us that his most celebrated publication was *Draught of Immortality*, and that he served as a member of the Calcutta Board of Customs, Salt, and Opium (later the Board of Revenue), they contain few other details. He is further described as the 'ornament of his service', 'an accomplished musician, clever draughtsman, fluent speaker, a versatile writer, [and] capital actor', 'in great request by the society of his day' (Buckland 1906: 329). Among attestations to his sociability, urbanity, and elegance of manners, a nineteenth-century anthology brought out in Calcutta commends him for the company he kept; many similar records of his social life, where the same names crop up in different combinations and permutations, may be found in the documentation surrounding Anglo-Indian society in early nineteenth-century Calcutta (Lawrence 1869: 89; Stark and Madge 1892: 18).

In one of these, Cedric Dover mentions that 'No dinner party of Parker's, it is said, was complete without Derozio, who added a gift for brilliant conversation to his youthful eagerness and charm' (Dover 1936: 110-11). Derozio, in his turn, addressed a tribute to him, 'Sonnet to H.M. Parker, Esq.', which concluded with a reference to the title of Parker's first volume of poems:

Bard of our sunny land, and golden sky!
My heart has gladden'd o'er thy magic lay!
Tis like the hymn of seraphim on high,
My soul hath drunk it—and it is to me,
Sweet bard! "a draught of immortality".[15]

Henry Derozio and Parker, then, regardless of race, were clearly friends, and both were also acquainted with Emma Roberts (*Oriental Scenes*, 1830), the first Englishwoman to write verse in India, and the first Bengali gentleman to write English verse, Kasiprasad Ghosh (*The Shair*, 1830).[16] Kasiprasad's admiration for Parker's first volume, *The Draught of Immortality*, is evident from a note, where he describes it as a 'beautiful Poem'.[17] Parker is mentioned again at the beginning of the third canto of Kasiprasad's title poem, 'The Shair', which is dedicated to him.

Derozio's *Poems* was published in 1827, the same year as Parker's *Draught of Immortality*. Reprinted a year later as *The Fakeer of Jungheera*, these were widely regarded in Calcutta as the work of a youthful genius, comparable to Chatterton (Lawrence 1869: 105), although a London reviewer complained of being 'continually reminded' of Lord Byron and Thomas Moore (*Calcutta Gazette*, 23 November 1829). Derozio identified himself as an Indian while he was editor of the *East Indian*, in which he strongly advocated the political rights of his race, and when he taught at the elite Hindu College, imparting a sense of nationality to the brightest Indian students there. His poems too, were famously nationalist in sonnets such as 'To India, My Native Land' and 'The Harp of India'. The anthologist, Lawrence, comments:

> He did not appear to see, as others did, that there was any merit in being descended from an English or foreign ancestry, and gladly assimilated himself with the ligitimate [*sic*] sons of the soil on which he was born. . . . ['East Indian'] had always been considered an obnoxious term, but Derozio rejoiced in it, and had no desire to be known by the more pretending and ostentatious appellation of "Eurasian," which his countrymen are so anxious to adopt, to trumpet forth, as it were, that they are half Europeans and half Asians. Derozio was content to be recognised only as a native of India.
>
> (Lawrence 1869: 103)

That such a self-conscious representative of the mixed-race community found a place at Henry Meredith Parker's dinner table, and constituted a distinguished part of an elite literary circle, is a testament to the cosmopolitan, entrepreneurial quality of East India Company rule in early nineteenth-century Calcutta. Writing in 1884, Thomas Edwards, Derozio's principal biographer, is surprised by the secular nature of Derozio's school, Drummond's Academy, from which he graduated at the age of fourteen, in 1823:

> It was one of the peculiarities of Drummond's school that, as in the Scotland of his day [when girls and boys studied side by side] . . . so in Dhurromtollah, 60 years ago, European, Eurasian and native lads conned the same lessons, and mingled together in the same school sports. (Edwards 1884: 12)

This intermingling between the races assumes significance in the general context of colonial relations, especially when compared to the conditions prevailing in India at the time of Kipling, writing in the last quarter of the century. Both poets caricature Indians, but the differences in their depictions reveal the deterioration of race relations between colonizer and colonized subject.[18]

Parker's racial attitude prefigures the race-thinking that, in a different incarnation, made Kipling a personification of the high tide of racism and racial theory. Edward Said, in his introduction to *Kim*, mentions racial theory as one of the reasons for Kipling's powerful influence on the culture of his time:

> But the other reason for his [Kipling's] power is that he was also supported by (and therefore could make use of) the authorised monuments of nineteenth-century European culture, for whom the inferiority of non-white races, the necessity for them to be ruled by a superior civilization, and the absolute unchanging essence of Orientals, blacks, primitives, women were more or less undebatable, unquestioned axioms of modern life. The extraordinary status of racial theory, in which it was scientifically proven that the white man stood at the pinnacle of development and civilization, is a case in point. (Said 1989: 30)

New research by historians on the British encounter with South Asia has emphasized what Irschick has called the 'dialogic' and 'heteroglot' nature of the interaction between colonized and colonizer in the first phase of British imperialism in India, pointing out that British racism was self-consciously constructed in the late nineteenth century (Irschick 1994; Trautmann 1997).

Bayly points out that 'much of the deeper social knowledge the European conquerors had once possessed withered away as expatriate society became more hierarchical and government more a matter of routine' (Bayly 1996: 365). Indians themselves were well aware of this deterioration in racial attitudes; Girish Chandra Ghosh, a leading Bengali journalist, wrote in 1862:

> Jones, Colebrooke, Wilson . . . respected our fathers and looked upon us hopefully at least with melancholy interest, as you would look on the heir of a ruined noble. But to the great unwashed abroad today, we are simply niggers—without a past; perhaps, without a future. They do not choose to know us. (Ghosh 1912: 434)

These changes find their literary manifestation in the writings of poets of Anglo-India such as Parker and Kipling, situated as they are in the historical process of changing British attitudes towards Indian civilization.

Parker mentions William Jones, John Shore, James Prinsep, and H.H. Wilson as being among the builders of the 'Empire of the Middle Classes'. He also demonstrates his affiliation with Orientalist scholarship in his first major publication, *Draught of Immortality*, whose narrative is taken from the *Mahabharata* and whose pages are populated by Hindu gods and goddesses.[19] In contrast, Kipling was enraged that William Morris included the

Mahabharata, 'that monstrous midden', in his list of 'the Hundred best books', for 'I can assure you that more hopeless, aimless, diffuse drivel (tempered with puerile obscenity) it would be hard to come across. . . . I wonder that he didn't stick in the Ramayana of Tulsi Dass and the Rig Veda to crown the lie.'[20] Writing in the last quarter of the century, Kipling is patronizing about Indians generally, but is especially vicious in his contempt for the educated Hindu, epitomized by the Bengali *Babu*.

Kipling's reductive theories of masculinity and admiration for men of 'action' reduced him to incomprehension when faced with the educated Bengali's reliance on free speech and the written word.[21] The caricature of the Bengali *Babu* in *Kim*, Hurree Chunder Mookerjee, who succeeds in his mission *despite* his nature, is a prominent example of Kipling's prejudices on the subject. These prejudices are revealed, in one instance, in the way the *Babu* insists on speaking English: 'That is all right. I am only Babu showing off my English to you. All we Babus talk English to show off . . .' (Kipling 1989: 231). Parker is not as rigid and ossified in his office as Kipling sounds several decades later; and although he too caricatures the Indian's confusion with the English language, he also portrays, even though ironically, the cosmopolitanism of the middle-class Hindu. Moreover, Parker does not predict, with anything approaching the same degree of delight, that mayhem will issue from the efforts of Bengalis to create change. Kipling, on the other hand, foresees that violence shall be engendered when Indians rule themselves in a poem such as 'What Happened', or in the short story 'The Head of the District' (Kipling 1994: 15; 1923: 131).

Kipling's views on the educated Indian in his published writings were in consonance with his personal opinions, expressed in his letters. An incident is related in one letter where his Punjabi clerk is upbraided for being '(and this hurt his feelings most of all) nearly as worthless as a Bengali *babu*.' In another, he is excited by 'A Bengali native paper, whose editor I would like to lick till he couldn't stand' for 'talking a lot of nonsense' about 'an extended movement on a national basis dealing with the primary education of womankind', for 'We might wait till Doomsday till the Bengalis educated their native women. . . .' This, when Bengal permitted women to enrol for graduate courses at the University of Calcutta in 1878, before any of the English universities. While reserving no affection for 'the semi-anglicised product of our Indian colleges who is hated and despised by Sikh, Hindu, and Mahommedan', Kipling's opinion is that the people of India generally 'have to be handled like children or young horses'.[22] In contrast, Parker reminds us that the Hindus are 'a people stubborn as Copts, deeply learned after their own manner, as versed in dialectics and as difficult to persuade as the Athenians of old, whom they resemble in subtlety'.[23] The degeneration of racial attitudes from the time of Parker to that of Kipling is most graphically illustrated through metaphor and analogy; Indians, once regarded by Parker as 'the Athenians of old', have been reduced, by Kipling, to the status of 'children or young horses', a deterioration Girish Ghosh foresaw when he mentioned being reduced from the status of ruined 'nobles' to 'niggers' without a past or future.

Apart from the innumerable clues in their published writings, then, it is the collation of personal attitudes as well, which helps us to differentiate between Parker and Kipling's attitudes on race, reform and colonization. Parker's humorous poem 'Young India', when contrasted with the larger body of Kipling's Anglo-Indian works, reveals a different intercourse between the British and the Indian, the colonizer and the colonized, an intercourse belonging to a more fluid time in the history of the British in India. Kipling's satire descends to Swiftian proportions, denying educated Indians, like the yahoos, the status of *men*, while in Parker's humorous verse, the ridiculous coexists paradoxically with his intimate knowledge of Bengali society, situating him in an 'insider's' position in relation to the phenomenon he describes. Consequently, Parker, in the poem 'Young India', is located neither properly within the tradition of canonical Western Orientalism nor, obviously, inside the parameters of Eastern 'mimicry', but in between these, in a grey area that is a relatively little-known offshoot of the imperialist enterprise.

NOTES

1. For key passages from Lord Macaulay's famous Minute on Education of 2 February 1835, see *Young*, 1952: 722.
2. Great Britain, *Parliamentary Papers, 1852-3*, Evidence of William Wilberforce Bird, 32: 237.
3. While the term 'Anglo-Indian' currently denotes a person of mixed English and Indian descent in India, it is used in this essay in its colonial context, meaning an English person who lived for a long time in India.
4. While the nomenclature is reminiscent of 'Young Italy', I could not trace any correspondence between the two movements, both roughly contemporaneous: Mazzini founded the patriotic 'Young Italy' movement in Marseilles in 1831, while Derozio died of cholera that year in Calcutta, aged 22.
5. According to Rajnarain Basu, Hindu College was known at this time by three names, Hindu College, Anglo Indian College, and simply, the College (Banerjee and Das: 1956, p. 44).
6. 'The native managers of the Hindu College were alarmed at the progress which some of the pupils were making under Derozio, by actually *cutting* their way through ham and beef, and wading to liberalism through tumblers of beer. From this new feature of Hindu education, the praise or blame of which must rest on the memory of Derozio, the managers dreaded the worst consequences. To put a stop to further in the science of *Gastronomy*, Derozio was dismissed in 1831. This is the plain unvarnished story' (Madge 1982: 42).
7. Wordsworth, *The Prelude*, Book First, lines 270-5 in *Romantic Poetry and Prose*, ed. Harold Bloom and Lionel Trilling, 1973: 192.
8. Works defending the character and nationalism of Young Bengal appeared simultaneously (Dutt 1848; Pal 1856).
9. My translation. Bankim Chandra Chatterjee, *Bankim Rachanavali*, vol. III, ed. J.C. Bagal (Calcutta: Sahitya Samsad, 1969), 139.
10. The sum of his political opinions was that the Indian Empire, 'The Empire of the Middle Classes', had been built by the spirit of enterprise intrinsic to middle-class English values. If Indians were interfered with by Bishops keen on conversion, or were to be governed by men in the British Parliament, that would spell the end of the Empire in India (Parker 1858: 11).
11. Cited in Leask 1992: 13. Byron's commercial instinct was sound; five years later Moore's *Lalla Rookh*, which had received a gigantic advance of three thousand guineas, became a publishing sensation in London.

12. Parker here prefigures Edward Said's contention, in *Orientalism* (1978) that the West has created the Orient through a process of selective representation, a concept that Parker precedes Said by more than a hundred years in labelling 'Orientalism'.
13. 'Gardens of gul in her bloom' sums up the preoccupation of that age with Persian poetry, 'gul' being the rose in the *gul-e-bulbul* legend of the rose and the nightingale, made famous by Byron in *The Giaour*: 'For there—the Rose, o'er crag or vale, / Sultana of the Nightingale' (Byron, 1981) 40, lines 21-2.
14. Parker's first work, *Draught of Immortality* (1827), however, was the opposite of prosaic; based on a theme taken from the *Mahabharata*, emulating William Jones's long poem, 'The Enchanted Fruit', it incorporated many Hindu mythological motifs and much Sanskrit etymology elucidated in footnotes. (William Jones, 'The Enchanted Fruit: or, The Hindu Wife: An Antediluvian Tale Written in The Province of Bahar,' *Asiatick Miscellany* 1 [1785]: 188-211.)
15. *Poems*, 119.
16. Moreover, Derozio proof-read Emma Roberts' volume of verse and saw it through the press, for which she acknowledged him in her preface (Roberts 1830: vi); while Kasiprasad wrote that Emma Roberts had 'expressed her wish to write an account of [his] life' (Long 1848: 510).
17. Ghosh 1830: 199.
18. This decline has been characterized by historian C.A. Bayly as a loss of what he calls 'affective and patrimonial knowledge' of Indian society, that is, 'the deep knowledge acquired by magnates with roots in the villages and the political sympathy which comes from ties of belief, of marriage and from a sense of inhabiting the same moral realm' (Bayly 1996: 65).
19. Themes from the *Mahabharata* predominated the first Orientalist publications in India: Charles Wilkin's *The Bhagvat-Geeta* was published in 1785, while William Jones' narrative poem, 'The Enchanted Fruit', based on a story from the same epic, appeared the same year in the *Asiatick Miscellany*.
20. To W.C. Crofts, 18-27 February 1886. Thomas Pinney (ed.), *The Letters of Rudyard Kipling*, vol. 1, London: Macmillan (1990), p. 121.
21. For a contextualization of this intolerance in broader social and economic processes, see Bayly, 1996: 314.
22. To Margaret Burne-Jones, [27] September 1885. *Letters*, 92; 28 November 1885-11 January 1886, ibid., 98, 100. For a discussion on 'the subsidiary homology between childhood and the state of being colonized which a modern colonial system almost invariably uses', see Ashis Nandy 1983: 11.

23. Parker 1858: 11. This essay blames the Mutiny of 1857 on the over-zealous efforts of missionaries and advocates instead an indirect route towards the establishment of the principles of Christianity in the people of India.

REFERENCES

Ahmed, Aijaz, *In Theory* (Delhi: Oxford University Press, 1994).

Banerjee, B. and S. Das (eds.), Rajnarain Basu, *Se Kaal Aar E Kaal* (1885), (Calcutta: Bangiya Sahitya Parishad, 1956).

Bayly, C.S., *Empire and Information* (Cambridge: Cambridge University Press, 1996).

Bhattacharya, Bhabani, *Socio-Political Currents in Bengal: A Nineteenth-Century Perspective* (Ghaziabad: Vikas Publications, 1980).

Biswas, Dilip Kumar (ed.), *The Correspondence of Raja Rammohun Roy* (Calcutta: Saraswat Library, 1992).

Buckingham, James Silk (ed.), *Oriental Herald and Colonial Review*, vols. 1-22 (London, 1824-9).

Buckland, C.E., *Dictionary of Indian Biography* (London: Swan Sonnenschein, 1906).

Lord Byron, *The Complete Poetical Works*, ed. Jerome McGann (Oxford: Oxford University Press, 1981).

Chatterjee, Bankim Chandra, *Bankim Rachanabali*, vol. 2 (Calcutta: Patra's Publication, 1983).

Derozio, Henry, *The Fakeer of Jungheera, a Metrical Tale; and Other Poems* (Calcutta: Baptist Mission Press, 1828).

Dover, Cedric, 'Henry Derozio: Eurasian Poet and Preceptor', *The Poetry Review* (1936), 27.2: 107-21.

Duff, Alexander, *India, and India Missions* (Edinburgh: J. Johnstone, 1940).

Dutt, Shoshee Chunder, 'Young Bengal or The Hopes of India,' *Essays on Miscellaneous Subjects* (Calcutta: Sanders, Cones and Co. 1854).

Edwards, Thomas, *Henry Derozio, The Eurasian Poet, Teacher, and Journalist* (Calcutta: W. Newman & Co. 1884).

Gandhi, Mohandas Karamchand (first published in Gujarati in 1927 and English in 1929), *An Autobiography* (London: Penguin, 1982).

Ghosh, J.C. (ed.), *The English Works of Raja Rammohun Roy* (Calcutta: Roy, 1885).

Ghosh, Girish Chandra, 'They Hate Us Youth', in M.M. Ghose (ed.), *Selections from the Writings of Girish Chandra Ghosh* (Calcutta: India Daily News Press, 1912).

Ghosh, Kasiprasad, *The Shair* (Calcutta, 1830).

Ghosh, Tapobrata, 'Literature and Literary Life in Calcutta', in Sukanta Chaudhuri (ed.), *Calcutta The Living City*, vol. 2 (Calcutta: Oxford University Press, 1990), 223-31.

Gupta, A. (ed.), *Studies in the Bengal Renaissance* (Calcutta: National Council of Education, 1958).

Irschick, Eugene, *Dialogue and History: Constructing South India* (Delhi: Oxford University Press, 1994).

Jones, William, 'The Enchanted Fruit: or, The Hindu Wife: An Antediluvian Tale Written in The Province of Bahar', in the *Asiatick Miscellany* (1785) 1: 188-211.

Kipling, Rudyard, 'Head of the District,' *Life's Handicap* (London: Macmillan, 1923).

——— *Kim* (London: Penguin, 1989).

——— 'What Happened', in *The Works of Rudyard Kipling* (Hertfordshire: Wordsworth Editions Ltd., 1994).

Lawrence, Thomas Benson *English Poetry in India, being Biographical and Critical Notices of Anglo-Indian Poets with Copious Extracts from their Writings* (Calcutta, 1869).

Leask, Nigel, *British Romantic Writers and the East* (Cambridge: Cambridge University Press, 1992).

Long, James, 'Autobiography of Kasiprasad Ghosh', in *Hand-Book of Bengal Missions*, Appendix D (London, 1848).

Madge, Elliot Walter, *Henry Derozio: The Eurasian Poet and Reformer*, 3rd edn. (Calcutta: Naya Prokash, 1982)

Mittra, Peary Chand, *A Biographical Sketch of David Hare* (Calcutta: Jijnasa, 1979).

Nag, Arun (ed.), *Satik Hutom Pyanchar Naksa* (Calcutta: Subarnarekha, 1991).

Nandy, Ashis, *The Intimate Enemy* (Delhi: Oxford University Press, 1983).

Pal, Kristodas, *The Young Bengal Vindicated* (Calcutta, 1856).

Parker, Henry Meredith, *Bole Ponjis: A Miscellany of Prose and Verse*, 2 vols. (London, 1851).

——— *The Empire of the Middle Classes: Being Nos 1 and 2 of Short Sermons on Indian Texts; Caste and Conversion: Being No. 3 of Short Sermons on Indian Texts, Concerning the Empire of the Middle Classes*; and *A Plan for the Home Government of India. With Provisions Calculated to Prevent or Limit the Evils and Dangers of Patronage* (London: 1858).

Pinney, Thomas (ed.), *The Letters of Rudyard Kipling*, vol. 1 (London: Macmillan, 1990).

Roberts, Emma, *Oriental Scenes, Dramatic Sketches and Tales, with Other Poems* (Calcutta, 1830).

Said, Edward, Introduction to *Kim*, by Rudyard Kipling (London: Penguin, 1989).

Sen, D.C., *History of Bengali Language and Literature* (Calcutta: Calcutta University Press, 1911).

Sen, Priyaranjan *Western Influence in Bengali Literature* (Calcutta: Calcutta University Press, 1932).

Sinha, Mrinalini *Colonial Masculinity: The 'Manly Englishman' and the 'Effeminate Bengali' in the Late Nineteenth Century* (Manchester: Manchester University Press, 1995).

Stark, Herbert A. and Madge E. Walter, *East Indian Worthies, Being Memoirs of Distinguished Indo-Europeans* (Calcutta, 1892).

The Calcutta Journal, or Political, Commercial and Literary Gazette (Calcutta, 1818-24).

Trautmann, Thomas, *Aryans and British India* (Berkeley: University of Berkeley, 1997).

Woodrow, Henry, 'On the Expediency of the Introduction of Tests for Physical Training into the Present System of Competitive Examination for the Army, Navy, and Indian Civil Service', in Colonel W.F.B. Laurie (1888), *Sketches of Some Distinguished Anglo-Indians* (London, 1875).

Young, G.M (ed.), *Macaulay: Prose and Poetry* (London: Hart-Davis, 1952).

Young, Robert J.C., *Colonial Desire: Hybridity in Theory, Culture and Race* (London: Routledge, 1995).

CHAPTER 6

'Young Turks' and the Kemalist Reforms: Continuities or Ruptures?

SAMIM AKGÖNÜL

The Turkish Republic justifies its foundation in comparison with the two oppositions: opposition to Western imperialism in its phase of armed struggle; and opposition to the authoritative monarchical system in its reformist phase. These two oppositions are distinct and provide the keys of not only the comprehension of the process of state but also of the national construction. However, while in the historiography of modern Turkey, the anti-imperialist sentiment of early Kemalism has been glorified, there is a denial of any link between the reform policies of the Turkish Republic and the reform introduced earlier in the Ottoman Empire. Consequently, it was unacceptable for the interpreters of Kemalist ideology to admit, that the roots of this ideology are deep, of which a part is to be sought in the Young Turks movement.

In this essay, first of all I will mention the facts to found the setting, then I will analyse some concepts of the kemalism whose origins are to be sought in the debates which animated the Ottoman society at end of the nineteenth century and the beginning of the twentieth century and finally I will try to present some personalities inseparable from Kemalism but who had close links with the Young Turks.

During the fight for independence, following the First World War, and thereafter at the time of the politicization of the Kemalists, observers pointed out to Mustafa Kemal and his former relations with the Young Turks. He felt obliged on several occasions to express his dissension with the latter and his distant feelings for them. From this point of view there is an explanation: starting from the end of the First World War, unpopularity of the Young Turk regime in the Ottoman Empire had reached its summit. The Sultan also supported this unpopularity. Thus shortly after the First World War, although the Young Turk movement was dissolved, three poles of the power disputed the favours of the people: monarchy, Young Turks and Kemalists. For the monarchists, to introduce the Kemalists as a continuation of the Young Turks movement was seen like the ultimate recourse against the rebels. This unpopularity and the will of the monarchists to influence the Kemalists were justified. The humiliating losses of the Balkan War and the First World War were presented as the failure caused by this regime. Indeed, the Ottomanism project had gone bankrupt. This utopian project, which was to create an Ottoman people on a citizen basis at a period when the nation-state started to be seen like the single remedy of imperialism, was in any case still-born. Having been diluted by Islamism, in other words to create an *umma* lacking a *millat*, was not enough partly because of Arab nationalism being born. However, the attempts at rescue of the Empire by the Young Turks movement were not limited to these two anachronistic ideologies. The third way of the trilogy of Yusuf Akçura, Turkism, was also conceptualized, but too tardily, too feebly and without a popular support. Nevertheless these failures, this unpopularity prepared the grounds on which the Kemalists would be able to blossom but without claiming the Young Turkism.

It is here where we touch a subtle point of this movement. This was definitely not monolithic, these objectives, these arguments and these actions vary according to time, the place and circumstances. These variations are at the same time vertical and horizontal. Vertical because the aspect of the movement has undergone major changes since 1856 when the association of the Young Ottomans, ancestor of the Young Turks movement, was founded, until 1920, the final fall of the Empire. These changes, which seem to be the circumstantial adaptations, make the Young Turks be accused of being pragmatist, not having an explicit programme, or worse—being opportunist (Ilhan 2004: 9-11). They are also horizontal because the Young Turks movement is divided into fractions, each of which follows appreciably different objectives with different means, which meet for such or such cause. The first nationalist Turks, their traditionalist opponents and even the first socialists come from their rows.

It should be specified all the same that to present the Ottoman Empire like a solidified regime without struggles for power and interest would be an error. From the early stage of its formation the regime adapted itself to the circumstances as the Ottoman State expanded and as its subjects diversified. But the true movements of reform in its modern meaning of the term started in the eighteenth century. The non-Muslim *millats*, in more increased contact with the Occident than the Muslims, were the first to encounter reformist ideas. Taking into account the increased economic means of these *millats* and the absence of a bourgeois class among Muslims, their members launched out in nationalist fights rather early, from the very beginning of the nineteenth century. At the same time, among Muslims of the Empire, particularly in the leading classes, a confinement to itself, a conservatism accompanied resistance to the independentist movements of the non-Muslims. This resistance itself was sometimes useful for the increasingly dogmatic Islam trying to stop any infiltration of the reformist ideas to Muslims (Karpat 1996: 31). In spite of the dogmatization of the dominant religion and an undoubtedly conservative will, one can say that it is in this century that the Ottoman elite became aware of a 'delay' compared to the Occident—a technical, economic delay but also a political delay. This idea of 'delay' in the nineteenth century was going to form the thought of the Ottoman elites and Turks and was going to lead to a Kemalist ideology, one of the bases of which was 'to catch up with Western civilization'. One cannot say that the Occidentalism, the modernism, and partly the secularism of the Kemalists find their roots in this awakening one century ago.

The first perception of the delay was realized at the military level and the first reforms inspired by the Occident were carried out in this field as of the eighteenth century. But these military reforms to some extent convinced the elites of the superiority of the Western system, in particular the French. Thus a climate favourable for reforms other than the military ones, was created in spite of conceivable resistances. This climate was able to blossom, relatively, thanks to the late formation of a bourgeois class among Muslim Turks. It is significant to note that all ideologists of the Young Turks movement, with the notable exception of Prince Sabahhatin, come from this new environment, like all of other Kemalist executives. These two groups often interlock with each other. Moreover, the educational reforms of the second half of the nineteenth century, in particular with the opening of the 'modern' schools like the College of Galatasaray (1868), allowed the development of a reformist intelligentsia, of Muslims and non-Muslims, open to the Western ideas.

Nevertheless these oppositional environments are not the only ones to understand the need for the reforms. Some enlightened sultans could overcome pressures of their conservative entourage to undertake significant restorations of the regime. Selim and especially Mahmut II are examples of this. It is during the reign of the latter, more precisely in 1838, that a step was taken towards a political citizenship levelling Ottoman, who announced the first steps of a secularization of the regime (Berkes 1993: 22 and *passim*). These rights to levelling tendency emerged in 1839 on an in-depth reform of the regime called *Tanzimat* (at the beginning of the reign of Abdülmajid), which would last until 1877. The *Tanzimat* decree, known under the name of *Gülhane Hattı Hümayunu,* granted equal rights to all Ottoman citizens without denominational distinction, promised an official protection for each individual but also taxation equality. We are here rather close to the idea of citizenship, which the Kemalists will use at the beginning of the twentieth century. However, the system of the *millats,* 'sophisticated' during centuries was not abandoned by *Tanzimat* at all as the Kemalists would do. On the contrary the non-Muslim *millats* of the Empire were due to this society regime with drawers and regarded it as essential for the independentist movements while accepting the levelling reforms about taxation. Thus, with regard to the project of creation of a political Ottoman nation, the reforms of *Tanzimat,* perhaps because they did not pass the barriers, had an opposite effect. Instead of bringing closer the non-Muslim *millats* of the Empire, they created the conditions facilitating their distance.

The *Tanzimat* decree reinforced by the *Islahat* decree (1856), encouraged by the Western powers for the protection of the Christians of the Empire, led to the drafting of the first Ottoman Constitution (1876). It is during this time that the Young Turks movement takes its roots with the 'Ottoman Youngs' who constituted a true opposition to the palate. The relative opening of the Empire to the Occident and the relative freedom of the press allowed the liberal transfer of ideas in the Empire through the emblematic figures such as Şinasi, Namık Kemal or Ziya Paşa. These enlightened young people, majority of whom were coming from rich families, had founded in 1865, a clandestine organization *Ittifak-ı Hamiyyet* in 1865. After an attempt of a coup d'état, which was aborted, they fled to Europe to found there, in 1867 the Association of the Young Ottomans in 1867. Admittedly the Association was dissolved in 1871, the year when the Sultan Abdülaziz established his authoritative regime. But it is with this first organization that the opposition movement, which was going to allow the constitutional regime of 1876, was launched. However the Young Ottomans had neither a solid ideology nor a definite programme (Bülent 1996: 51-5). Contrary to the conservatives who saw bad points in the freedoms of *Tanzimat*, they appreciated it. But they considered that these reforms were superficial, imposed by the foreign powers and asked for liberal reforms in-depth. They criticized the absolutism of the Sultan, the economic forfeiture, the *vis-à-vis* dependence of foreign powers, the political and economic foreign interventions, which would be principles of the Kemalists thereafter. But they were also against the equality between Muslims and non-Muslims, at least in its application, which they considered in discredit of the Muslims. Among the proposals of the Young Ottomans one could see that patriotism was expressed for the first time explicitly. It was this new idea that would develop the Kemalists a few decades later. But the patriotism of the Young Ottomans, contrary to that of the Kemalists, was to be one of the values, which accompany fidelity with monarchy, and denominational unity. It is disconcerting to see that the Young Ottomans showed that they did not believe that the non-Muslims could be animated by patriotic feelings with regard to Ottoman State. This idea would be used by the Young

Turks but also by the Kemalists. And finally they were always these Young Ottomans who claimed a constitutional regime, following the example of occidental monarchies as well as the creation of an assembly of representatives of the Ottoman people. But more than that, the first discussions on the concepts of the Republic, national sovereignty and the individual freedom (passage of the subject to the citizen) are in the writings of Namık Kemal and Ziya Paşa (Lewis 1988: 152-5). The Kemalists will prepare writings to conceptualize the republican system. The Kemalist transformations are thus accomplished to make it possible (as it is repeated in all the Turkish constitutions since that of 1924) to the Turkish people to rise to the level of 'civilization', as the Young Turks executives claimed it. By doing this, whatever the brutality and the suddenness of measures taken were, the majority of them took the projects, reforms or at least of the debates which had marked the last decades of the Ottoman Empire again.

However, the similarities should be differentiated. Contrary to the Kemalist movement, this one did not have a popular solid base. One cannot say that the proclamation of the constitution in 1876 wasn't a result of popular revolution. It is a fact that the executives of the Young Ottomans were in Paris and London, whereas Kemal was himself in Anatolia most of the time. Nevertheless, although they were away from the base, the conjuncture was favourable for the reforms. Their determination to reform, a certain idea of Ottomanism on the new Sultan Abdülhamid II and the pressures of the foreign powers made the proclamation of the constitution possible in 1876. Although it was abolished a year afterwards by a Sultan of an authoritarianism without precedent, this constitution was going to be used as a basis for all Turkish constitutions since the beginning of the twentieth century. Indeed, the transformation of the regime, of absolutism into a constitutional monarchy was in the long term to allow the abolition of the system of the *millats*, which the Kemalists will make a success of a half-century later. But for the moment, the nationalist movements crossing the Christian communities of the Empire who had created a movement of react-ion among Turks with the birth of Turkish nationalism, made that the idea of Ottomanism was emptied in terms of its meaning.

Nevertheless when we look closely at the constitution of 1876, which was to remain theoretically in force until 1918, one is struck by the 'modernity' of certain articles. The essence of this constitution lay in the crisis in the society in the last decades of the Empire; it raised many questions, which the Kemalism was to solve thereafter. For example, the first article proclaims that the Ottoman State is an indivisible unit, this indivisibility will be recalled and used in all of the Turkish constitutions but also in the national pact proclaiming the war of independence (1920). It is enough to replace the term *Devlet-i Osmaniye* with Turkey to obtain the same meaning. Other principles, like individuality of the rights (Article 6) or the national representation (Articles 60-1) will be preambles for the later constitutions.

It is the abolition of this first constitution, which has its roots in the transformation of the Young Ottomans movement into a true opposition to the despotism under the denomination of Young Turks. The first secret organization of opposition to the Hamidian regime was founded in 1889 (*Ittihad-i Osmani*) by taking the model of the Italian *Carbonari*. The movement was radicalized in 1895 by reaction to the Armenian nationalist movement and was transformed into a secret association: *Osmanlı İttihat ve Terakki Cemiyeti* (Ottoman Committee of Union and Progress). As Turkish nationalism is reactionary, the 'nationalist' organizations are also reactionary. The first activities of the association were propaganda, in particular in the military and student environments. Propaganda sheets such as *Osmanlı, İntikam, Kanuni Esasi*, but especially *Meşveret*, spread liberal ideas and claimed the return of the constitutional regime. The editorials of *Meşveret*, witness the discussions around new concepts like secularism, national sovereignty, equality of rights, etc. Nevertheless these discussions show many hesitations. Like the Young Ottomans, the Young Turks did not have well-defined doctrines either. Although these ideas are discussed in the publications of the movement, the women's rights, secularity, or social equality were shown like positive concepts, all the executives presented after-effects of Islamism and conservatism. The economic ideas were also stripped of depths, the first economic steps of Turkism was taken certainly to show itself, but the principal idea was all the same—the safeguarding of the Ottoman State in its multiple components. With this intention, and it is perhaps the only point on which all the Young Turks agreed, they estimated that the re-establishment of the constitutional monarchy was necessary and sufficient. Ottomanism was defended and provided that the Ottoman State does not suffer from it. A naïve idea, which suggests the fraternity of all Ottomans, was the starting point of the paradoxical concepts of the Ottoman nation and the Ottoman fatherland. The principal objective wasn't freedom but safeguarding the State. It is in this sense that the Kemalists will dissociate Young Turks, while changing the objectives towards the foundation of a new State in rupture with the Ottoman State, which was cherished by the Young Turks so much. Despite everything, even conceptualized in a chaotic manner, a Turkish nationalism was also born among Young Turks. According to the individuals, there was an exclusive nationalism, which is strongly tinted with Islamic values, and for the first time in the Ottoman Empire, the Turkish language starts to occupy a significant place here. This tendency to refer to the language, which will be taken and developed by the Kemalists, is widespread in the literary circles close to the Young Turks.

It is for the first time that we see in the editorials of *Meşveret* the concept of 'fatherland', not attributed to all of the Ottoman territories but to Anatolia. The Kemalists will use the same concept in the national Pact in 1920 to mobilize the Anatolian Turks.

Young Turk opposition thrived abroad, particularly in Paris. It is in this city that the second congress of the Young Turks was held in 1907, gathering all fractions of the movement, in particular the group of Prince Sebahattin (those who defend individual enterprise) and the Unionist ones (those who want an extremely central state). The conclusions of the Congress called the Ottoman people with various types of resistance, of the strike of the taxes to the boycott of the local elections. It is interesting to note that the true success of the disputes took place in the Balkan regions of the Empire, mainly in Macedonia, where the dispute gained an identity of a mass movement. All Roumelia, and the area of Mustafa Kemal, a young 27-year-old officer in 1908, was shaken by demonstrations. Hundreds of telegrams sent to the palace invited the Sultan to restore the constitution. It is impossible to think this liberal movement didn't impress only Mustafa Kemal, inspector of the railway line Thessaloniki-Skopje in 1908, which was traversing the area. The opposition movement spread particularly by the medium of young officers in addition to the middle class and civil servants. This is why the proclamation of the second constitutional monarchy must be differentiated from that of 1876. This time, there wasn't a coup d'état at the palace but there was indeed a popular dispute (Tanör 1996: 111). The success of the movement had shown that the popular mandate belonged to Mustafa Kemal. Another characteristic of this success, and not the least, was its non-bloody aspect. The Sultan had been constrained to proclaim the constitutional monarchy without a civil war with the support of all the denominational components (for different reasons) of the Ottoman population.

The new constitutional regime felt a necessity to amend the Constitution of 1876. In this respect, the 21 modified Articles formed to some extent a new Constitution (1909). With these modifications, hereditary monarchy was confirmed and theocratic aspect of the regime was even reinforced. However, the monarchical capacity was limited considerably by a parliamentary power. But the true changes in this new Constitution were in the field of the individual rights. More freedom (Article 12), more equality between the citizens were aimed to create a political Ottomanism.

One can say that it is since this period that the Young Turks become a true political power claiming to direct the Ottoman State and tending to choke various forms of opposition. The political branch of the Young Turks, the Committee of Union and Progress, seized the power gradually, was radicalized and established an increasingly authoritative capacity. Unpopularity of the movement coincides with this seizure of power and develops with the Balkan wars and the First World War. The movement disappeared with the Ottoman defeat in 1918.

From Empire to Republic

In the foundation of the Republic, the Kemalists were to present themselves in rupture with three former poles of power: monarchy, theocracy and Turkish Young Parliamentarism. Actually, these three poles of power will inspire the Kemalist regime with various degrees. But in so far as the objective was 'modernization', the Kemalists presented themselves in total rupture with them.

When we take into account the totality of Kemalist practice, continuities are striking. Even the most spectacular, the most revolutionary, or the most surprising modifications that people regard commonly as innovations, thus those concerning the cultural fields and, or the question of the language and the writing or the statute of the woman or the question of the legal enclaves, weren't absent from debates which agitated the Ottoman elites of the Young Turks era.

For example, one of the most radical measurements of the Kemalist reforms was abandonment of the Arabic alphabet for the profit of the Latin alphabet and this was done with an aim to occidentalize the Turkish society. The objective, which had not been admitted, was to mark the rupture with the Ottoman society more. But this idea to deeply transform the Arabic alphabet used by Ottoman Turks, and to even give it up for the Latin alphabet was often evoked by these young Turkish thinkers in the intellectual mediums where also tendencies aiming to reduce the Arab and Persian grammatical and syntactic forms appeared which Osmanli tended to abuse (Lewis 1988: 121). The linguistic reform was not a Kemalist invention. Simply, the latter had courage to make it and still more to emphasize the reform with a purification of the Turkish language, sometimes in an artificial manner, to make it one of the cements of the Turkish nation. Hunting down the foreign words since the beginnings of the Republic, Mustafa Kemal did not only aim the 'return to pure Turkish!' but he also tried to erase any trace of the Ottomans.

Another example relates to the emancipation (sometimes forced) of the women and the transformation of family values. The first steps of this will of the occidentalization of the status of woman are visible as of the time of *Tanzimat*. Ways of life inspired from the Occident developed, and the second constitutional period witnessed an acceleration of this process in the large cities of the Empire: multiplication of girl's colleges, proliferation of female associations, women coming to the public places such as theatre, park, and even demonstrations without veil. These changes of the female condition, although they were marginal as they were not related to the campaigns where the majority of the Turkish women lived, took root so much that when the Swiss Civil Code was adopted which included the abolition of polygamy, the voting rights and the eligibility granted to the women, it did not have radical opposition demonstrations.

Thus 'modernization' and 'occidentalization' were not exclusive Kemalist practices. Several generations of Ottoman reformers had preceded them, beginning delicate debates of society by sometimes considering similar transformations without carrying them out completely: attempts of synthesis of modernity and Islam, more or less radical inclinations of occidentalization or integrist reactions rejecting too hasty imports of foreign models (Marcou 2000). In spite of the elitist and urban aspect of these reflections, a modernist effervescence preceded without question the fall of the Empire including the most significant field—that of religion.

Continuity was more concrete in the field of law. Since the *Tanzimat* era, several legal changes have been borrowed from the Western models. Ditto for the field of public law, where the first measures taken at the time of *Tanzimat* are related to technical subjects: police headquarters with the installation of ministries in Western regions, the territorial organization with the law on *Vilayet*, the administrative law for Council of State inspired by the French model, public finance with a reorganization for better management of the debts, etc. This occidentalization of law brought double paradoxical process. While one part of the Ottoman elites, especially of the leading class (mainly diplomats and high-ranking military, two mediums of predilection of recruitment of the Young Turks and the Kemalists), were also Westernized in their traditions, another intellectual group—writers, journalists and scientists—became more and more attached, reaction, conviction or opportunism, with the Islamic tradition and savagely opposed the 'imitations'. Opposition between the reformers and the traditionalists born in the Young Turks era continue in the Republic until now. Admittedly, it is often difficult to make this distinction explicit as the individuals change 'side', follow reforms for certain fields and traditions of another.

This opposition between reformers and traditionalists must be more differentiated. Certain groups of Young Ottomans and Young Turks but also thereafter of the Kemalist executives tried in the same way until today, to propose solutions to erase this dichotomy between Islam and modernity. Among Young Turks some sought to work out a synthesis of Islam and Western constitutionalism. The influence of the ideas of the French Revolution, which was probably increased by the laic spirit which it conveyed, should not be neglected either to explain the turn which is more political than the Ottoman reformism. Admittedly, under the command of Kemal Atatürk himself, there were anticlerical sometimes anti-religious measures taken in the Republic and, but it is useful to point out that in the first years of the national fight, Mustafa Kemal leaned on these religious mediums, which supported the belief that they were going to save the Caliph. After the death of Mustafa Kemal, a rather radical return of religion also initiated by the old Kemalists. This religious return continued until the 1980s when the Turco-Islamic synthesis devoted the Islamic religion (Sunni-Hanefi), as one of the components of modern Turkish society.

The Ottoman Constitution of 1876 (compiled on the basis of the Belgian Constitution of 1831) makes Islam a religion of State (Article 11) while recognizing the freedom of religion as well as many civil laws making all Ottomans equal in front of the law (Article 16). One should not forget that this Constitution was implemented after several decades of debate and reforms during which the Empire had radically changed to approach the forms and the structures of the European States.

It is during the oppositional period that the Young Turks, a new generation of reformers, draw more radical reforming claims but resolutely secular ones. But dominated by its very influential nationalist wing in the army, the Committee for Union and Progress, the Young Turks after 1908 gave to the reform practices a centralizing and authoritative aspect. This branch of the Young Turks, admirers of the French Revolution, very much influenced by positivism, wanted to abolish the system of the *millats* definitively and to make an Ottoman citizenship emerge guaranteeing equality in front of law and ignoring religious differences. It was thus a question of establishing a communautarist society based on ethnico-religious nationalities to support the advent of a modern nation-State, which is one and indivisible, equalizing, uniform and rational, rather close to what the Kemalists will realize thereafter. This doesn't mean that the Ottoman reformers hadn't thought of going ahead in the secularization of the system. They have simply and perhaps involuntarily prepared the ground, completed 'their work of sapping' allowing the radical reforms, but without the force of the Kemalists it was impossible to abolish the Caliphate to emancipate women, to prohibit the religious brotherhoods or to change the alphabet. The reason lies in the objectives—the Young Turks wanted to preserve the Empire, and the Kemalists wanted to found a different regime, the latter profited from the favourable international context, which witnessed the collapses of the great empires.

It is necessary to see the audacity and the courage of the Kemalists for not only they dared to be against the Allied Power to gain a war of independence whose result was very dubious at the beginning, but also they were able to impose on the Turkish society in rather radical and also rapid manner to accelerate its mutation in a vertiginous manner. The victory permitted Mustafa Kemal to have the prestige necessary for the legitimization of his action and the Ottoman reformers hadn't had this advantage: to be able to register its reforms within a new official framework. The proclamation of the Republic gave the Turks a nation-state reformer, rather than a new political regime (Marcou 2000).

The Elites

In 1918, with the Ottoman defeat, the official apparatus was in place. The civil servants of the Empire, the diplomats but also the provincial executives of the ancient regime adapted themselves rather quickly to the Kemalist regime. It should be said that the new leaders of Turkey didn't follow a policy of recruting. There hadn't been a systematic replacement of the senior officials of the Ottoman regime by others. Rational explanation of the recovery of this apparatus by the Kemalists resides in the shortage of intellectuals in the Turkey of 1923, who were able to retake the direction of the country from the starting point. The great majority of those, which represented the Ottoman State in 1918 abroad, became representatives of the new Turkey; the local authorities, the teachers and the other groups of civil servants put their competence at the service of the new State. Some among them, by opportunism or conviction, were transformed into bold cantors of kemalism.

But the implication of the Young Turks is not limited to the mass of the civil servant of the late Ottoman period. Several emblematic figures of the beginnings of the Republic came from the Young Turks movement, with the astonishing and sometimes completely contradictory positions.

Among these figures, in addition to Mustafa Kemal himself, it is necessary to mention some personalities like Ziya Gökalp (born in 1876 in Diyarbakır, a Kurdish province), one of the intellectual guides of the Young Turks. He integrated the Committee for Union and Progress in 1985 when he incarnated the intellectuals, following the example of Prince Sabahattin. After significant official and educational functions within the Young Turks government, he was exiled in Malta after the defeat. It is in 1921 that he returns to Diyarbakır and behaved like one of the enthusiastic defenders of the Kemalist fight. In 1922, even before the proclamation of the Republic, the Kemalists nominated him in an academic mandate within the Ministry of Education. He was very traditionalist, strongly attached to the values of Islam, and after his death (1924) he became the symbol of the Islamist Turks considered as an anti-Kemalist.

In the antipodes of Ziya Gökalp, always resulting from the Young Turks' rows, one can find intellectuals such as Şefik Hüsnü, Sadrettin Celal, Mustafa Suphi or Ethem Nejat who converted into socialism. Whereas Sadrettin Celal and Şefik Hüsnü were influenced by Jean Jaurès, Ethem Nejat followed the German Spartakists and the most known among them, Mustafa Suphi, had become an admirer of the Bolsheviks. Regarded as one of the fathers of Turkish socialism, he was born in Giresun, which is a province with a strong orthodox concentration, in 1883. After studying law, he obtained a doctorate in sociology from Sorbonne where he came in close contact with the exiled Young Turks. With the return to the Ottoman Empire in 1910, he had close links with the Unionists, but since 1912, when the latter came to power, he started to loosen his contacts with them. Badgered because he was against the Balkan wars, he escaped to Anatolia in Russia. In Batoum he formed a close relationship with the Bolsheviks. After the revolution, he organized the first Turkish Congress of the Socialists in 1918 and took part in the foundation of the Turkish Communist Party in Baku. He also supported the national Kemalist Movement of 1919-20 with other Turkish Communists. At the end of the war of Independence, in 1921, he was invited to return to Turkey by Mustafa Kemal along with his 14 comrades, but he was assassinated on his way.

These two opposed figures, cherished at first by the Kemalists and diabolized later, are two characters that have become the references for anti-Kemalists thereafter. But among the close collaborators of Mustafa Kemal, we see individuals who collaborated actively or who simply supported the Young Turks movement. Among these we can mention the case of Celal Bayar, one of the prime ministers of the Turkish Republic, and the third president of the Republic. This civil servant and banker of the late Ottoman period, who was born in Bursa in 1883, was very active within the Community for Union and Progress since 1909 to such a point that he became the general secretary of this movement in Izmir. The case of Kazım Özalp is similar. He was born in the Balkans (1880). The minister of defence of Mustafa Kemal in 1924 and thereafter president of the National Assembly, he became one of the significant executives of the Young Turks in Thessaloniki in 1906, where the movement was strongest and where Mustafa Kemal had his first contact with the reformists. Fethi Okyar, a close collaborator of Mustafa Kemal, another prime minister of the Republic, had been the General

Secretary of the Committee for Union and Progress in 1913. Previously he had been the military attaché of the Young Turks in 1908 in Paris. Other more or less known figures, who were to form the skeleton of the Kemalist executives thereafter are Mazhar Müfit Kansu (1873-1948), Ömer Naci (1878-1916) and Tevfik Rüştü Aras (1883-1972) who were in the epic Young Turks before. Yunus Nadi Abalıoğlu (1880-1945), one of the spokesmen of the Kemalism through its *Cumhuriyet* (newspaper), which is still in circulation and remains nowadays as one of the bastions of radical Kemalism, had been the head redactor of the Rumeli newspaper in 1910, which is a publication attached to the Committee for Union and Progress. In 1911 he had even been appointed in the Ottoman parliament.

These examples illustrate that the Kemalists of the first rank, as those who would be the heads of other current policies of contemporary Turkey, had close or far relationships with the Young Turks movement and this included Mustafa Kemal himself. One can't say that this movement of three decades was a good political school, about disputes at first and about the exercise of the power thereafter. In this school, all the political communities of the Republic of Turkey started up, while taking care to dissociate themselves thereafter.

Conclusion

Do the Kemalist reforms constitute 'a successful repetition of the Young Turks revolution'? Admittedly, the conditions under which the Kemalist reforms proceeded are not the same ones as those surrounding the initial reforms and changes, which were partially carried out thereafter by the Young Turks. But in this field the Kemalists and the Young Turks had something in common: opposition to the Sultan. The Young Turks were opposed to him by claiming a constitutional parliamentary system and without evoking the abolition of the Sultanate explicitly; the Kemalists aimed at proclamation of the Republic until the final action. The Young Turks thought of saving the Empire but the Kemalists thought of putting an end to it.

Another difference remains in the duration—the Kemalists had to move quickly, without thinking whether social evolution of the population of Turkey was sufficient or not to welcome the radical reforms (replacement of the *fez* with the hat, for example) whereas the Young Turks didn't have neither the necessary authority nor time because of the successive wars.

And finally, let us render unto Ceasar the things which are Ceasar's. Without the personality, the charisma, the authority or the will of Mustafa Kemal radical reform as that of Mustafa Kemal could not have been achieved. And it forces us to note that the Young Turks movement was multicephalic, lacking a charismatic leader as Mustafa Kemal.

REFERENCES

Berkes, Niyazi, *Atatürk ve Devrimler* (Istanbul: Adam, 1993).

Bülent, Tanör *Osmanli-Türk Anayasal Gelismeleri* (Istanbul: Afa, 1996).

Ilhan, Atilla, *Hangi Laiklik* (Istanbul: Is Bankasi Yayinlari, 2004).

Karpat, Kemal, *Türk Demokrasi tarihi* (Istanbul: Afa, 1996).

Lewis, Bernard, *Islam et Laïcité: la naissance de la Turquie moderne* (Paris: Fayard, 1988).

Marcou, Jean, 'La laïcité en Turquie: une vieille idée moderne', in *Confluences Méditerranée*, no. 33, 2000.

CHAPTER 7

The Young Iranian Society

KAVEH BAYAT

In the early years of the twentieth century, when the emergence of a diverse range of 'Young' movements, such as the Young Turks, the Young Bukharans, etc., represented the advent of a progressive movement in the East, in Iran which was also experiencing similar developments in the shape of a Constitutional Revolution, no 'Young' movement of consequence took shape. The term 'Young Persians', or to be more precise *Jeune Persans*, is frequently mentioned in some of the foreign reports of the Constitutional Revolution of Iran (O'Connor 1931: 135), but as a matter of fact, at the peak of these events, when the movement was 'young', this term, with parallel events in Turkey and elsewhere had only a vague descriptive disposition and did not take an organizational form. It was only at the end of this period, i.e. in the early 1920s, when there were almost no traces left of the original 'Young' movements of the East, that a group of young Iranians who had recently finished their education in Europe and returned to Iran established an organization called *Jami'at-i Iran-i Javan*, or the Young Iranian Society. Although this Society had a relatively long life—up to the late 1970s—it enjoyed political prominence only for a brief period of time, in the mid-1920s.

This brief period of activity in the mid-1920s and the Society's emphasis on the 'moral regeneration' of Iran that it intended to achieve through an intensive educational programme and the way in which the society endeavoured to realize this programme in conjuncture with other political forces of Iran, is the main subject of this paper.

The pattern of *modernity* and *progress* in contemporary Iran has experienced a very diverse and disparate line. It took a long time to understand and comprehend its various components and a much longer time to give substance to a general will towards the necessity of its implementation. After the end of the First World War, when there was an end to a long period of foreign intervention, Iran finally found an opportunity to act for the implementation of a series of reforms that it had strived to realize in previous decades but had failed to for various reasons—including the constant meddling by imperial powers. At this juncture in Iran, modernity and progress were no longer in need of further justification. They had already become a public demand. What was required was a concrete definition of modernity and a series of practical measures for its implementation—a task that was mainly relegated to a collection of young Iranians who had just returned after studying in Europe.[1] For a period of time, 'the Young Iranian Society' took the lead in this regard.

In the late December 1921, a group of young and educated Iranians such as Aliqoli Khan Mohandes al-Dowleh, Hassan Khan Shaqaqi, Isma'il Khan Mer'at, Javad Khan Ammeri, Hassan Khan Nafissi, Mahmud Nasseri, Mohammad Vahid Tonekaboni and Ali Akbar Siassi proclaimed the establishment of the Society of the Young Iranian, a society whose membership was specifically restricted to those young Iranians who had studied in Europe. An obvious '. . . mark of friendship and a common attention to the European civilisation . . .' was reported by the *Ittihad* newspaper, as the foremost characteristic of this group (*Ittihad*, Joza 29, 1301). Beside a final clause on the need for '. . . the rejuvenation of the Iranian economy by all possible means', the promotion of cultural, artistic and sportive activities amongst the youth formed the main items of the original programme of the Society (*Ittihad*, Hamal 30, 1301). Although most of the early actions of the Society were confined to such activities as the staging of a number of satirical plays, organization of musical concerts, and also a series of public lectures on cultural and economic topics that revealed the non-political nature of the Society, but early on it was deemed necessary to re-emphasize this point; on 20 June—ten days after the inauguration of the Society—in an announcement published in the *Ittihad* newspaper, after a re-run of the original programme, the 'Committee' of the Society declared that they do not '. . . meddle in any type of activities related to politics'(*Ittihad*: Saratan 8, 1301). By and large in the early stages of its existence, the Society kept its word and was mainly engaged in cultural activities.[2] Even though on certain occasions, such as the election for the fourth and fifth parliament—spring of 1921 and winter of 1924—it published its list of candidates, it was only in 1926, after the publication of the Society's weekly paper *Iran-i Javan* (*The Young Iranian*) that it decided to assume a marked political disposition (Siassi 1968: iv-v).

The abolition of Islamic courts, emancipation of women, revitalization of public spirit, and an attempt to adopt the 'noble ingredients of the occidental civilization' were among the points discussed in the Society's new agenda. Beside some other demands—such as the abolition of capitulations, a revision in custom tariffs for the benefit of national industries and agriculture, construction of a railway network in Iran—that were very much in vogue in those days, the programme's comprehensive clause on national education was quite distinct (ibid.).

'We are for those resolute persons and young ideas who believe Iran is for the Iranians and also believe that one has to work hard to achieve one's ideals; those who believe that for deliverance there is no way to pursue, but the path that others have taken' (*Iran-i Javan*: no. 1, 1927). This introductory notice published in the first issue of the *The Young Iranian*, despite its brevity, is a telling description of the world-view of the Society. First of all, if there was going to be any results, it could only be achieved through the efforts and endeavours of 'resolute persons and young ideas', a social force that the Society was going to mobilize. The emphasis on the necessity to follow the 'path that others had taken', i.e. the path that the West had taken, was the second important point mentioned in this note.

For Ali Akbar Khan Siassi, a psychology graduate from Paris, who could be considered a leading figure of the Society, a massive and long-term educational programme was an essential prerequisite for the formation of such a bright, young and determined generation:

The main source of our predicament lies in the moral traits of the members of the society. Even if you manage to establish the best system of administration, borrow the best possible laws and legislatures from abroad and adopt them, eventually it is those same members of society that have to run that administration and implement those laws, their moral shortcomings are bound to overshadow all those endeavours.

Deficiencies such as idleness, hypocrisy, indifference to religious and moral values '. . . that are all symptoms of this malady, are no secrets . . . they had been dealt with by other writers in so many instances, but instead of offering solutions they have mainly confined themselves to lamentations . . .' (ibid.: no. 3, Esfand 20, 1306).

Moral Degeneration

For Ali Akbar Siassi the moral malady of society could be classified into two groups; the deep-rooted and traditional maladies, and a series of modern afflicted ailments in the previous fifty years of dealings with the West.

'Lack of purpose, or as westerners call it lack of "ideal", which could be a symptom of the first type of those ailments, has made us all . . . old and young, learned or illiterate, as hopeless and pathetic as decrepit elders, it has made us lose all signs of life and vitality.' According to Siassi, this category of ailments had three causes; first of all the superstitions that had been foisted upon Islam. The present-day Islam is not '. . . the sacred principles that in the early centuries of manifestation gave rise to the resurgence of many Nations, that led a host of primitive tribes onto the path of civilisation, established great states. . . . It fundamentally differs from its original and genuine principles.' The second cause of the present situation was '. . . the course of history, with it's incessant waves of foreign invasions, repeated defeats, and absolute monarchies, that has made us all accustomed to sycophancy and adulation . . .' and finally the literary heritage of Iran:

. . . Those bygone poets and writers of whom we are rightfully proud since we are well aware whatever esteem and respect that is left to us is because of them, but at the same time we have to admit that their works were more in line with the beliefs and values of those days. Their literary heritage has had an important impact on the moral identity of people and it is through the sweet and pleasant tone of these poets, that running like pure water that the roots of superstitions, Sufism and sycophancy are reinforced. (*Iran-i Javan*: no. 5, 1306)

The second set of disorders, that is to say those that the Iranian society has been afflicted through its recent dealings with the West, are mainly evident in a discernible lack of self-confidence, '. . . a sense of disability to act in an independent manner' (ibid.: no. 5). Of course, this malady, coupled with a certain disdain towards the moral values of a society that expresses itself in an infinite greed for the superficial symbols of modernity such as new cars and costumes '. . . is not the source of this decadence, but only an added factor to a susceptible entity'. It is because of these susceptible grounds that '. . . novel disorders get easily accepted and one of the reasons why we are much more liable to imitate the errors of the Europeans, rather that their positive moral values' (ibid.: no. 50, 1928).

To resist this onslaught, 'we had to be in possession of certain skills that we lacked, and in order to acquire these skills, we had to stage an educational revolution. A comprehensive programme for the education of the young generation. But those who had to educate us for this new life '. . . both our religious and temporal leaders, took no appropriate step in this regard [and] all of a sudden, without the least of preparations, we stepped into a new world . . .' (ibid., no. 49, 1306).

Since education could not be confined to mere literacy, but had to be attained through the moral and physical education of the young generation, for the Society nothing could be worse than the duplication and development of the present educational system. It was not enough to just keep complaining about the dour conditions of education in Iran, a set of practical measures had to be implemented and first of all the whole system had to be renovated (ibid., no. 3, 1306). For this purpose one had to train enough teachers and educators: 'By a series of conditions and a definite programme, a group of our compatriots had to be selected . . . and sent abroad both to be educated and to experience a moral and ethical transformation and also to learn how to educate . . .' it is only after the return of this group that we could have enough teachers and educators for our primary schools (ibid.: no. 52, 1306).

It is in the further elaboration of the practical side of this programme that the other aspect of the Society's outlook, its emphasis on taking 'the path that others have taken' finds a definite form. Modernity is something that has to be acquired from the West, and for this acquisition it is necessary to go there and to live there. And it was not only in the field of education that the Society was of the opinion that one has to take such a direct approach. Mirza Hassan Khan Nafissi in an article entitled 'The Deficiencies of Iran and the Obstacles to its Economic Progress', discussing the 'lack of experts in different branches of science and industry' and the need to send off students abroad, made, it clear that '. . . five or ten persons are not enough. In order to transform the economic feature of Iran in just a few years, thousands of Iranians have to go abroad every year . . .' (ibid.: no. 38, 1306).

Dispatch of students abroad and having an educated cadre at hand as a precondition for any sort of modernization was the credo of the society. For example, a Bill was proposed in Parliament by Sayyid Hassan Taqizadah to send ten students abroad every year to study railways and metallurgy (ibid.: no. 10, 1306).

When Mirza Ali Akbar Khan Davar, Reza Shah's Minister of Justice in an attempt to reorganize the ministry, proclaimed its dissolution in the winter of 1926, the Society was not sure about the outcome. Recourse to an adequate and educated cadre was the only means of ensuring the success of such a bold programme. '. . . If ten years ago the Minister of Justice had thought about this project, we would never have had to resort to the dissolution of the ministry today . . .' and now that it has been dissolved the chances of success are slight '. . . because the number of our legal experts and law graduates are relatively limited . . .' (ibid.: no. 10, 1306).

In other fields of development, the Society was of the same opinion; whether it was the question of the reorganization of the Ministry of Finance and the Society's emphasis on the need for the hiring of foreign advisers (ibid.: no. 16, 1306), or certain specific issues such as the construction of a railway network in Iran which had to be launched on foreign investment (ibid.: no. 2, 1305; no. 9, 1306; no. 13, 1306; no. 27, 1306).

As it was discussed, a marked stress on the experience of the West—'the path that others have taken'—formed the hallmark of the Society's world-view. But this emphasis, in no way could have been interpreted as an appeal for an overall Western domination. Hassan Nafissi's articles on the need for a comprehensive revision of the present customs tariffs for the benefit of the nascent industries of Iran (ibid.: no. 4, 1305; no. 5, 1306; no. 27, 1306) or the question of Iranian oil revenues (ibid.: no. 48, 1306) that were both assuming important positions in the politico-economic debates of the day, had in mind the reinforcement of the nations economic independence. In the field of education too—the speciality of the *Society*—the strengthening of national values was very much in mind; Isma'il Khan Mer'at, devoted part of an article to explain what he regarded as the essentials of National Education (ibid.: no. 5, 1306) on the absolute imperative of the foundation of special colleges for the training of teachers as a pre-condition to any change or reform in the educational system.

In comparison to certain other political beliefs of the time, lack of any xenophobic tendencies could be considered a main characteristic of the Society, whether in the field of education, where the Society was critical about the restrictions imposed by the Ministry of Education on the activities of foreign missionary schools in Iran, or when it came to its views on world developments.

The Young Iranian was very keen on political developments around the world and the position of Iran in this regard, and in every issue had one or two detailed and analytical articles—usually by Mohssen Re'is—on these subjects; The League of Nations, events in neighbouring countries, and current developments in the Soviet Union in a series cf articles by Ali Soheili (ibid.: nos. 1-17, 1305-6) events in Iraq (ibid.: No. 21, 1306; no. 31, 1306), Arabia (ibid.: no. 36, 1306), and Turkey (ibid.: no. 30, 1306) were among the topics discussed in the pages of *The Young Iranian*.

The Limits of Success

Although the Society's achievements as a forum for a coherent set of policies and proposals for the cultural and political development of Iran was remarkable, its success as an independent political group was insignificant. As in the case of most political parties in Iran, rather than political programme or ideology, it has always been a certain personal allegiance that essentially has served as a pivot of collaboration, for the Society of the Young Iranian it was definitely its world view, a direct and explicit move towards Westernization. The Society's '. . . reluctance to pursue individual interests and private motives . . .' (ibid.: no. 42, 1306), and its deliberate policy to not get '. . . impressed by day to day and trivial events . . .' which was thought to be one of its main reasons of success, had its obvious draw-backs too. 'Individual interests and private motives', or to be less ironic, the polity that was more identifiable by its political leaders and the ideas they represented, was an essential and inseparable part of Iranian politics and the 'day-to-day and trivial events' were the real background through which these individual and private motives were pursued.

Years later, when recounting the Society's attempts to participate in the parliamentary elections of the mid-1920s, Ali Akbar Siassi admitted that their approach to politics had been unrealistic. During the 1926 elections, when Ali Akbar Davar, the leader of the Radical Party, had proposed an electoral coalition and the Society had stated they would only accept this offer on the condition of the Radical's firm undertaking 'not to' collaborate with '. . . other groups, and especially the conservative merchants and Muslim clerics who are totally opposed to the programme of the Young Iranian Society . . .', Davar had retorted that at the present time '. . . the conservative classes form the majority of the society and without their support it is impossible to win elections, hence, for the moment, they had to leave aside revolutionary ideas and concentrate on securing parliamentary and ministerial positions . . . at any price, and then to tackle the question of basic reforms.' Siassi wrote, '. . . for us who were a group of earnest young men, this course of action didn't sound right, and even though we sensed that he was right, we rejected his offer of cooperation and initiated an electoral campaign as an independent group; Davar and his followers won and we were defeated' (Siassi 1968: v).

As a matter of fact the Young Iranian Society, like other intellectually-inclined groups in modern Iran, despite a very well-defined world-view and an impressive ability to express these views, was unable to create a suitable political apparatus to pursue its goals. Although at this period the Society considered itself a political group and had '. . . the establishment of a parliamentary regime and principles of democracy, the protection of individual freedom and the right to free expression . . .' as its main goals (*Iran-i Javan*, no. 1, 1305) but in comparison with the active role it played in educational and economic issues, when it came to politics, it failed to make any significant contribution. As mentioned earlier, despite the Society's political veneer and occasional attempts to participate in elections, in the early 1920s, when it was at the zenith of its political activities in Iran and the fate of many political issues of vital importance was being decided, it showed more interest in cultural and artistic endeavours and when in 1926—with the publication of its weekly newspaper—the Society finally made a serious attempt to act as a proper political organization, it was too late and the issues had already been settled.

The Young Iranian Society held a totally different view from some other Iranian groups, such as the Radical Party of Davar, which from the outset was for an authoritarian mode of modernization—something they eventually found in the person of Reza Shah (Bayat 1993: 116-33). Ali Akbar Siassi in one of his last articles in *The Young Iranian*, in a sharp criticism of 'those people . . . who think when the majority of a society has sunk into ignorance and moral deprivation and is unable to recognise its own interests and manage its own affairs . . .' it needs a guardian, and '. . . it is the responsibility of that guardian—in complete disregard of their desires or individual freedoms—to force them on to the right path . . .', pointed out that the colonial powers too in the justification of their aggressive policies resorted to the same arguments. For him this type of policy contained two major shortcomings; first of all '. . . more than ninety-five per cent of these powerful guardians work out to be a bunch of greedy crooks . . .' and secondly

> . . . this method too, like similar means, such as sermon and lectures or the enactment of special laws . . . can only leave some superficial results behind and will never be able to penetrate the character of the individuals or transform their personalities . . . even if an enlightened despot materializes and succeeds in performing certain improvements, it is not going to improve the plight of the society and eventually people are going to be left alone with their own miseries . . . [because] it is only the superficial aspects of the society that they manage to transform not the reality. Therefore the moment there is a deterioration of power or the slightest sign of a crisis or revolution, all of a sudden and in an extreme form, the real state of the situation, with all its ills and corruption, re-emerges. The futility of punishment or terror is one of the basic principles of education. . . . (*Iran-i Javan*, no. 28, 1306)

For the Young Iranian Society '[t]o diagnose the ills of society and to show the practical means for their treatment' was their main task and the 'implementation of these means', main task of the state. Although they seemed to be well aware of the futility of coercion in this regard, they did not elaborate in what manner the state was to implement their proposals.

As mentioned earlier, at the height of disputes and political confrontations about this crucial question in the early 1920s, i.e. the desired characteristics of a capable regime, the Society had other matters in mind, and when it decided to take up a prominent political role, the issue had already been settled. Now in the figure of Reza Shah, Iran had an 'enlightened despot' who was set to succeed in what the Constitutional Revolution of Iran had failed to deliver: The modernization of Iran.

At the outset, there didn't seem to be any problem; the Society had a well-defined programme and had also declared that it was '. . . only going to support a government that was ready to act for its [programme's] full implementation . . . '. But it didn't take long for the Society to find out they didn't have much of a choice. In the Summer of 1927, Teymourtash, Reza Shah's powerful Court Minister in a probable imitation of similar developments in Italy or Turkey, came upon the idea of creating a single, all-inclusive political party; Hezb-e Iran-e Now, or the New Iran Party. According to R.H. Clive, the British Minister in Teheran: 'The idea was to create a strong party with branches all over the country, and primarily, it was to be a party grouped around the person of His

Majesty [Reza Shah], which would do his bidding with the utmost loyalty' (Persia, Annual Report, 1927: 118).

In September 1927, at a special assembly that was held at the Society's club, it was announced that after two months of negotiations with the representatives of the Iran-e Now party, in order to reach a 'unity of purpose and a common programme', the Society has decided to join the new party. As Teymourtash had elaborated in the speech he delivered at that assembly,

> ... because the progressive forces of the country are small in number and scattered, and as a result, do not have the power to resist the united front set up by the reactionaries, they usually have to give in, now that under the banner of the progressive Kingdom of His Majesty, the ground is suitable for the advance of modern ideas, it is the duty of all progressive elements to leave aside minor differences and unite in a joint effort to drive the country towards progress and civilisation. ... (*Iran-i Javan*, no. 28, 1306; *Ettela'at*, no. 296, 1927)

But the Society did not join Teymourtash's party; after a fortnight, the *Young Iranian* reported, they could either declare the dissolution of the Society and join the new party, or '... find a way to preserve the Society and at the same time—as far as it is possible—to meet the demand of the new party.' The first option was out of the question, because

> ... the *Young Iranian* is a well established Society, with a reputation for patriotism and impartiality throughout the country and as a matter of fact has become the only source of hope for the progressive elements of the country ... [and] as the only regular force confronting the massive might of the reactionaries, it has proved its capabilities and for that reason, to dissolve it is akin to the betrayal of the cause of progress and modernisation of Iran.

Given that the Society didn't want to reject this offer as not to be accused in the future that '... there was only one way of salvation for Iran and that way was blocked by the Society ...' it decided on a 'third way'—the Society would be declared a non-political group

> ... so each one of us—as long as the interests of the country dictates—could independently devote our energy, with utmost sincerity for the advance of the cause and cooperate with the new party. If to our absolute joy, our aspirations were attained in this manner, the better; and if one day we found that the goals of this party differs from the aims of our Society ... then we

will decide to change course and make a new decision. In that case, once again the Young Iranian Society will step in to pursue its unfinished aims by other means. (ibid.: no. 30, 1306)

The autocratic Pahlavi regime which was rapidly gaining ground, greatly simplified the issue; members of the Society did not have a hard choice to make because in a few months time even Teymourtash's attempts to create a single and comprehensive party collapsed and the Iran-e Now party was disbanded. This futile act's only practical result was to put an end to the independent existence of some other political groups of the time such as Davar's Radical Party or Taqizadah's Taraghi group which after dissolving themselves in order to join the new Iran-e Now party had no chance to pick up where they had left off (Persia: Annual Report, 1927). The Young Iranian Society, by the 'Third Way' it opted for, managed to survive Reza Shah's reign as a non-political society, and in an individual capacity it didn't take long for most of its members to achieve prominent positions among the elite of Iran—Ali Akbar Siassi became a high ranking official in the Ministry of Education; Hassan Nafissi, a prominent economist; Javad Ameri, Ali Soheili and Mohssen Re'is all attained important positions in the Ministry of Foreign Affairs; Isma'il Mera't was named Minister of Education; Mostafa Qoli Bayat, Hossein Amin and Ahmad Adl all became high ranking officials in the Ministry of Public Works (Aqeli 2001: 212, 702-3, 838-40, 845-6, 984-5, 993-4, 1406-7, 1599-1600).

As for the question of the compatibility of the goals of the Society and the goals of the emerging regime: 'If to our absolute joy, our aspirations were attained in this manner, the better; and if one day we found that the goals of this party differs with the aims of our Society . . . then we will decide to change course and take a new decision[. . .].' For a long period of time—almost fifteen years—nobody was allowed to 'decide on a change of course', and when after the invasion of Iran by the Allies in 1941 and the collapse of the autocratic regime of Reza Shah, such an opportunity occurred, the remnants of the Young Iranian Society were not very eager to address these types of questions. To explain this reluctance, one can draw attention to their too well entrenched position in the ruling elite of Iran or the fact that they were not as 'young' and vigorous as they used to be, but the truth of the matter is that the Society of the Young Iranians despite its occasional political pretensions had never really been a political organization. As mentioned earlier, at the height of the political disputes and confrontations of the Iranians on a range of crucial issues such as the alleged deficiencies of a democratic way of development or the assumed merits of autocracy in this regard, the Society had other matters in mind and when it decided to take up a prominent political role, the well-established position of Reza Shah had already settled all the disputes and confrontations.

After the demise of Reza Shah's regime, the remnants of the Young Iranians who still had retained some sort of an organizational structure, made some attempts to revitalize the Society as a political organization. In 1943, they even managed to restart the publication of the *The Young Iranian*, but the situation was totally different from what it had been in the early 1920s. In the post Reza Shah era that was still reeling from the effects of his coercive modernization, issues such as modernity and the best ways of getting *modernized* that used to be the domain of the Young Iranians was not that important any more and in addition Iran was going through an acute political crisis and the issues it had to tackle were much too serious and critical for this kind of groups to deal with. As a result, after a short period of time, once again—and this time for good—the Society decided to give up politics and revert to what really suited them; that is to carry on as a social club, with a reputable restaurant and occasional cultural and scientific lectures, something they did up to the late 1970s.

NOTES

1. For a brief account of the lives and works of some of these students see Delfani (1993: 14-51).
2. A series of public lectures, concerts conducted by some young and innovative musicians as Ali Naqi Khan Vaziri, a variety of 'Moral' plays that were regularly staged in Teheran's fashionable Grand Hotel, such as Hassan Moqadam's *Ja'far Khan az Farang Bargashteh* (Ja'far Khan who has returned from Europe), that was a tremendous hit . . . were of particular

importance in this period of the Society's activities. See 'Preface' (Siassi 1968: I-IV; see also (Azhand 1994: 113-14).

REFERENCES

Azhand, Ya'ghoub, *Namayeshnameh nevissi dar Iran* (Play Writing in Iran), Tehran: Nashr-e Ney, 1373[1994].

Delfani, Mahmud 'Mohasellan-e Irani dar orupa dar tool-e jang-i jahan-ye avval' (The Iranian Students in Europe during the First World War), *Ganjinih-yi Asnad*, Tehran, vol. 3, nos. 10-11, Summer-Autumn 1372 (1993).

O'Connor, Frederick, *On the Frontier and Beyond* (London: John Murray, 1931).

Siassi, Ali Akbar's 'Preface', in *Majmoo-yi Sokhanraniha-ye Kanoon-e Farhangi-ye Iran-i Javan* (The Collected Lectures of the Cultural Centre of the Young Iranian), vol. 1, Tehran: Kanoon-e Farhangi-ye Iran-e Javan, 1347 (1968).

Iran-i Javan, no. 1, Esfand 5, 1305 (24 February 1927).

——, no. 2, Esfand 12, 1305 (3 March 1927).

——, no. 3, Esfand 20, 1306 (11 March 1927).

——, no. 4, Esfand 27, 1305 (18 March 1927).

——, no. 5, Farvardin 5, 1306 (25 March 1927).

——, no. 9, Ordrbehesht 2, 1306 (22 April 1927).

——, no. 10, Ordibehesht 9, 1306 (29 April 1927).

——, no. 13, Ordibehesht 30, 1306 (20 May 1927).

——, no. 16, Khordad 20, 1306 (10 June 1927).

——, no. 21, Tir 24, 1306 (15 July 1927).

——, no. 27, Shahrivar 4, 1306 (26 August 1927).

——, no. 28, Sharivar 11, 1306 (2 September 1927).

——, no. 30, Sharivar 25, 1306 (16 September 1927).

——, no. 31, Mehr 1, 1306 (23 September 1927).

——, no. 36, Aban 6, 1306 (28 October 1927).

——, no. 38, Aban 21, 1306 (12 November 1927).

——, no. 42, Dey 2, 1306 (23 December 1927).

——, no. 48, Dey 30, 1306 (19 January 1928).

——, no. 49, Dey 7, 1306 (28 December 1927).

——, no. 50, Dey 14, 1306 (4 January 1928).

——, no. 52, Bahman 28, 1306 (17 February 1928).

CHAPTER 8

Ganj Azer against the Soviet Rule in Azerbaijan

SOLMAZ RUSTAMOVA-TOHIDI

The modernization of Azerbaijani society that started in the second half of the nineteenth century was slightly different from similar processes that took place in other Muslim countries of the Orient. Following two consecutive wars with Iran in the early nineteenth century, Russia finally succeeded in annexing the southern Caucasus, including today's Azerbaijan, to the Tsarist Empire. The Azerbaijanis had at first felt that being citizens and not enjoying equal rights, but just as an ethnic minority, whose language, religion, traditions and culture, to say nothing of other civil rights and freedoms, might be violated by the ruling nation with impunity. It was this circumstance that stepped up processes of intra-ethnic consolidation and development of the national self-consciousness among the Azerbaijanis.

As for the national self-consciousness of the Azerbaijani, it would be appropriate to adjust for complexity and contradictoriness of historical part of its formation. As a Muslim society Azerbaijan for centuries was part of the Persian Empire, in close contact with the Islamic world and at the same time neighbours with Christian countries, oriented toward the Western culture. Such an advantageous location of the country at the intersection of the East and the West made it possible to adopt democratic values, common for both cultures.

On the other hand, the development of capitalist relations in Azerbaijan in the second half of the nineteenth century led to radical transformation of the social structure of Azerbaijani society, sophistication and growth of intra-national economic relations and shaping of the unified national market. Hence, there sprang up an economic base for processes of ethnopolitical consolidation, which finally resulted in the new ethnic character of the Azerbaijani nation.

In the period under consideration, a local intelligentsia emerged, designed to meet the intellectual and ideological needs of the major social groups of the Azerbaijani society. Despite its small number, the local intelligentsia played a key role in Azerbaijani people's realization of its social, political and national rights. Representatives of the Azerbaijani intelligentsia, educated in the central cities of Russia, Turkey and Iran, compared their people with more advanced peoples, imbibed ideas of national liberation and democracy and thus contributed to the cultural, educational and political progress of society, accelerated shaping of the Azerbaijani nation. It is quite natural that the Azerbaijani intelligentsia placed itself at the head of the national movement. It is no mere coincidence that political leaders of the Azerbaijani national movement came from ranks of the intelligentsia.

Thus, rapidly growing social, political, economic, cultural and intellectual advances that began to move in Azerbaijan after its joining the Russian Empire earlier in the nineteenth century, ended later in the same century with the shaping of the Azerbaijani nation as a historically predetermined ethno-social group. As a rule, shaping of the nation blends with the creation of a state organization to ensure its sustainability. It was the aspiration of the Azerbaijani nation being shaped that accounted for the emergence of the Azerbaijani national movement in early twentieth century.

Historical experience is illustrative that national movements in various countries worldwide, given the diversity of their goals and tasks, forms and methods of struggle, experience two mutually related stages. The stage of immediate struggle for political independence, as the second, the supreme step in the development of national movements is always preceded by the first initial stage, characterized by the domination of national-cultural reasoning. The hallmark of the first stage in all national movements is a severance from the pre-capitalist ideological and cultural heritage and a transition to the principles of the new national ideology, theoretically based on the prospects of ethno-cultural and political development of the nation.

It has to be kept in mind that at the initial stage, the ideologues of national movements worldwide dealt with the problems of culture, development and improvement of the national language and its consolidation in the literature, propaganda of the folk character of art, creation of a new system of fiction, education of national sentiments, i.e. of spiritual values, which ideologically reflect the shaping of nation and the nation's self-consciousness. The said features were typical for the initial stage of the Azerbaijani national movement that covered late nineteenth century until the February Revolution of 1917 in Russia. It would be appropriate to recall that the Azerbaijani national movement in the period under review symbolized the struggle for the development of the national language and culture, aimed to attain a national equality within the Russian Empire, since administrative and legal restrictions arising from the Tsarist legislation impeded the free national development of Azerbaijani. However, scale and results of this struggle proved to be rather impressive: creation of Europeanized literature, plays, press, theatre and even opera in Azeri, establishment of the principles of renovation, modernization of philosophical and social thought of Azerbaijan, struggle against clericalism and religious fanaticism, against feudalism and Eastern despotism, drafting of the new alphabet to replace the Arabic one, opening of European-style schools (*usuli jadid*), development of science and education in Azeri and, finally, putting forward in the foreground a question of national identity. During this period, the ideology of the national movement was shaped based on 'Turkicization, Islamization and modernization' slogans. The first symbolized an ethnic originality of Azerbaijanis; the second pointed to the religious affiliation and solidarity with other Muslim struggles against colonialism; the third implied adherence to civilian democratic values. These factors make it possible to lead the processes happening in Azerbaijan in the reviewed period outside the limits of a specific movement, titled as 'young', in the classical sense of the word. Through initiators and subsequent followers of the process were representatives of the young generation with ideas and conceptions, new for the Eastern society, large scale, many-sidedness of trends, ideologies and forms of this movement make it different to identify Azerbaijani intellectuals with their counterparts not only in Turkey and Iran, but even Muslim regions of the Russian Empire. Examining national and cultural processes, typical for Azerbaijani in the end of the nineteenth century and beginning of the twentieth century, Wimbush noted that 'this awakening and accompanying mental ferment was a local Azerbaijani phenomenon, and not a mere imitation to Russian cultural patterns, characteristic of Povolje Tatars' (Winbush 1979: 65).

The victory of the February Revolution in Russia in 1917 resulted in the qualitatively new situation to immediately influence the nature of the Azerbaijani national movement. Its major goal was to fully eliminate the national and colonial oppression and exploitation, foreign sway, and to gain independence, i.e. realize the right of the Azerbaijan nation to self-determination. The second stage of the national movement was notable for its own goals and tasks, methods and forms of struggle. Whereas the first stage of the national movement focused on the national press, activities of cultural and education institutions, various public organizations, on activities in different representative bodies of the Russian empire, the second stage concentrated on the struggle with political parties as the basic centres of the national movement.

Formed in top secrecy in 1911, the Musavat (Equality) Party emerged from the underground straight after the February Revolution. During this period, the political programme of the party shifted from the concept of Islamic unity to the struggle for the national rights of Azerbaijanis and other Turkic people thanks largely to theoretical works of the leader and founders of the Musavat Rasulzadeh party. Leaders of the party realized that powerful and truly independent state in Azerbaijan might be established on democratic values only. It is no mere coincidence that the principal slogan of the party was 'freedom, independence, democracy'. This was a turning point in the political evolution of not only the party but the entire Azerbaijani national movement. Despite ideological and political diversity of forces in the national movement, as well as multiplicity of political parties, it was the

Musavat which placed itself at the head of the Azerbaijani national movement and headed the struggle for the establishment of an independent state in May 1918. Since this essay is not aimed at the history of the Azerbaijan Democratic Republic (ADR), let us focus on the factors which predetermined the emergence of the 'Young' movement in the Soviet period of the Azerbaijani people.

Despite the defeat of the national movement because of foreign invasion, its achievements were so brilliant and significant that it affected the subsequent development of the Azerbaijani society. Note that the establishment of the ADR marked the advancement of the Azerbaijan nation as the first state in the Muslim and Turkic world based on Republican principles of government. Under the direct guidance of the leaders of the national movement, a society was created with a wide range of democratic freedoms and political pluralism. The democratic nature of this society openly manifested itself against the background of the neighbouring Muslim countries where predominated the eastern despotism with all its attributes. The implementation of the national movement programme enabled Azerbaijan to appreciably outstrip its neighbouring Muslim countries by the sheer level of its democratic development. Crucial and progressive changes took place in the economic, political and cultural life of the country in the two years of ADR rule. These changes positively influenced the strengthening of national self-consciousness and dignity among the Azerbaijanis.

On 28 April 1920, the National Government of Azerbaijan, existent just for 23 months, was overthrown by the 11th Army of Soviet Russia and the local Bolshevik organization. The Soviet power put an end to the national independence of the country, gained after toppling of the Tsarist monarchy in Russia, February 1917. The Sovietization of Azerbaijan and establishment of a one-party system based on the ruling Communist ideology, was received negatively by the local population, especially the national intelligentsia, who sized it up as the restoration of previously Russian, and now red-coloured, domination. The national liberation forces started its campaign for separation of Azerbaijan from the USSR. Insurrections broke out in towns and villages of Azerbaijan lasting several years; strikes in industrial centres of the Republic were mercilessly suppressed by the Soviet regime, followed by mass arrests of the representatives of political parties, national and public organizations and the intelligentsia. Opponents of the new power had to change their methods of struggle and go into hiding to proceed with their resistance. A part of the leadership and activists of the Musavat Party, formerly the ruling party of Azerbaijan, succeeded in avoiding arrests, executions and exiles, and migrated mainly to Turkey and Iran, where they managed to publish their party's periodicals and pursue their anti-Soviet activities. Faced with cruel repressions arranged by the new regime, the national forces had to resort to methods of underground activities.

Starting from the mid-1920s, the Musavat Party was actively and consistently involved into gaining sympathies of the Azerbaijani students. The Central Committee of Musavat distributed in 1925-6 among all illegal Party branches a document titled 'Program of education of youth of non-Party'. This political line was championed by teachers, the party members and those unrelated to Musavatists, pro-nationalists, formerly employed in all the areas of public education, especially pedagogical schools and some higher educational institutions. These teachers drew up a special curriculum, especially in literature, history, geography, etc., to raise the national consciousness among the youth.

It has to be kept in mind that the education of youth was just a first step in the creation of necessary prerequisites for drawing the Azerbaijani youth into structurally organized activities aimed at combating the Soviet power and preserving national values. Next came a second step—to create circles and groups of nationalistic-minded students, directly related to Musavat and engaged in certain social and political work. However, soon after the activities of Azerbaijani teachers became a focus of attention of Soviet state apparatus which introduced a strict surveillance in all the areas of social and political life of the country, including the public education system. Arrests started among the teachers. Suffice it to say that 54 teachers from various regions of Azerbaijan, charged with the realization of the said programme, were arrested in 1927 (CSA file 27, sh.167). As is shown in the materials of the Azerbaijan

State Political Department (ASPD), 'this figure is just a beginning, the real situation is much more deplorable' (CSA file 27, sh. 167).

It should be noted that it was the lack of necessary teaching staff, Communist-minded national cadres, as repeatedly stated in ASPD document, that impeded mass repressions against suspect teachers (ASPD, file 27, sh. 167). In an effort to avoid society's open discontent, leaders of the Republic, primarily made of non-Azerbaijanis, recommended ASPD 'to carry out gradual sending off, of hostile elements, and then submit to the Central Committee of the Azerbaijan Communist Party a list of Turkic teachers' (CSA file 29, sh. 162).

Despite the measures taken, authorities failed to hamper the strengthening of nationalistic sentiments of the Azerbaijani youth, fed by systematic activities of Azerbaijani teachers in the second half of the 1920s. An eloquent testimony to the fact were tens of illegal youth organizations, circles and groups, operating in the reviewed period. Suffice it to mention that ASPD uncovered and liquidated 12 organizations between 1926 and 1929, composed of students and teachers, who acted on the 'political instructions of Musavat'(CSA file 73, sh. 51-5).

Among the most distinguished organizations there was *Ganj Azer* (Young Azer). The history of its origin and activities is a typical example of sentiments, the aspirations and potentialities of the young generation of Azerbaijanis in the 1920-30s. Thus, far from professional political struggle, the Azerbaijani students of Baku Pedagogical College were often engaged in discussing the recent past of their country when Azerbaijan had been headed by prominent state and public figures, who carried on a political line, absolutely different from the Communist one, aimed at improving the status of the Azerbaijanis and their native language—Turkic, etc. These young people gave priority to reading and examining works of Azerbaijani poets and writers, especially those whose poems were permeated with national spirit, full of protest against foreign domination and glorified the 'heroic past of Azerbaijan', and spoke of 'freedom and independence'.

Enjoying particular popularity was the famous Azerbaijani poet Ahmed Javad who often resorted to allegories in his verses.

Azerbaijanian students tried enthusiastically to decipher a hidden meaning in his works. The most active members of this student group were Hasan Aqa Akhundzadeh, Gasim Aslanov and Ali Aqa Aslanov who were children of peasants. They finished the first grade Soviet school in 1925-6 and entered a pedagogical college of Baku. In other words, their origin and education were fully consistent with the requirements as set forth by the Soviet State to serve a stronghold of the new power, seeking to train its own cadres. Following the arrest of these students, the documents emphasized that they came not merely from the poor peasantry, but also high ranking peasantry (CSA file 27, sh. 171). Such was given as an explanation of the fact how young people with communist education, who were also members of the Young Communist League, suddenly became ardent nationalists and fought against the communist regime. Punitive organs of Azerbaijan linked mass involvement of Azerbaijanian youth into nationalistic ideas to the existence of strong nationalistic sentiments among Azerbaijanian intellectuals, including teachers.

Heads and members of Ganj Azer had to recognize the influence of their teachers in shaping their views. An eloquent testimony to the fact are fragments from Aslanov and Akhundzadeh statements: 'One day a teacher of the Turkic literature Atababa Musakhanly touched upon the responsibilities of teachers in the countryside' by saying:

> At one time, Germany was under the yoke of France. Some people believe it was Bismark who, thanks to his political far-sightedness and diplomatic skills, allegedly delivered his country from the French. No, it was German village teachers who, due to their indefatigable efforts among masses, gave a powerful impetus to the development of national self-consciousness of German peasantry. The same honorable duty is incumbent upon you as future teachers. (CSA file 27, sh. 169)

Referring to the historical facts from the German history was also another teacher of Baku Pedagogical College, and a former member of the Ittihad Party, Nur Mamed Shahsuvarov: 'You must learn Russian not to become Russified but to adopt their great culture, just as at one time Germans, having learnt the French language and culture, overthrew the French' (CSA file 27, sh. 169).

Numerous documents of ASPD shed light on Ganj Azer activities and confirm that Azerbaijani teachers referred to the history of not just European countries. In an attempt to educate their pupils in the national spirit, these teachers focused on the history and literatures both of Azerbaijanian and Turkic peoples as a whole: 'When I studied at the school, a teacher of geography often deviated from the topic, and focused on heroism of Turks, their campaigns, victories, conquests, etc.' A teacher of literature, Mamed Zaki Dursunzadeh, for two years, told us about Turkic history:

> One day Emin Abid read us a story titled "A bomb" by a certain Turkish poet Omar Sadraddin. The nature and topic of the story were counter-revolutionary. Amin Abid offered his congenial pupils to read works of Pan-Turkist poets. (CSA file 27, sh. 168)

It should be added that in the period under consideration, the history, literature, geography, etc., curricula were supervised in a strict manner the authorities. In particular, any reference to the history of Azerbaijanis was strictly prohibited.

However, one cannot ignore the influence of teachers in awakening the interest of youth in the national history and literature. It was Atababa Musakhanly's advice that helped future organizers of Ganj Azer be carried away with works of prominent Azerbaijani poet Ahmed Javad, whose prohibited verse 'Gek Göl' (Blue Lake) gave them an impetus to further their activities. Thus, Gasim Aslanov, one of the leaders of the organization, confirmed that:

> When I and Hassan Aqa Akhundzadeh were sitting in Sabir public garden in 1925-1926, discussing a verse of Ahmed Javad Gek Göl, Nasir Mamedov came up to us. He was a nationalist, and joining our conversation, pointed out that when saying Gek Göl the poet meant the oil industry of Azerbaijan, seized by Russians. We often met since then, and every time he stressed that Azerbaijan had been a colony of Russia. (CSA file 27, sh. 173)

Gradually these young intellectuals came to share their views with like-minded persons in an organized way.

'As a group of students, ideologically and politically close to each other, we entered Baku Pedagogical College in 1925-6. We got together and talked about the national matter, etc. Our group was composed of persons we intended later to organize into our 'three' following the establishment of Ganj Azer. (CSA file 27, sh. 172)

It would be appropriate to note that all the data on the establishment and activity of Ganj Azer are based on materials of ASPD. As distinguished from later 1930s during Stalin's repressions when enemies were summarily liquidated and people had to implicate each other and plead guilty of invented, improbable crimes, the situation was slightly different in the 1920s. According to ASPD documents on Ganj Azer:

> It was logic of group activity that urged them towards organized forms of work. After they familiarized themselves with Musavat Party's experience of work, each of them came to the conclusion of the establishment of illegal organization of young Musavatists. The program of this Party was fully consistent with their anti-Soviet, nationalistic aspirations.
>
> (CSA file 27, sh. 173)

In so doing, young students decided to get in touch with Musavatists and follow their advice before establishing their own organization. Two of them—Gasim and Ali Aqa Aslanovs—appealed to the librarian of Buzovna village, near Baku, Ali Alizadeh, who often gave the students anti-Soviet literatures. At the same time, Hassan Ali Akhundzadeh appealed to his stepfather Mesih Akhundzadeh who did not even try to conceal his nationalistic sentiments. As active members of an illegal Musavat organization, both of them welcomed the plans of the young people, gave them useful advises as stressing the necessity of the establishment of the organization to comply with Musavat party principles, i.e. a cell to be composed of three persons (CSA file 27, sh. 173).

Following a long-term preliminary work, both Aslanov and Akhundzadeh met in the summer of 1927 in Mardakyan and held a constituent meeting. As a result, a central 'three' of illegal organization of young Musavatists was set up under the name Ganj Azer, with its own programme and charter. A purpose of the establishment of the organization was defined as follows:

> By calling Azerbaijani students to join
> the Ganj Azer and later promoting them
> to join Musavat Party, the Musavatists aim
> to secede from Soviet Union and join Turkey,
> a land which is not stands only as the political
> and spiritual magnet for all-Turks,
> but the entire Muslims of the Orient. (CSA file 27, sh. 174)

To accomplish the goal, the Ganj Azer should:

> establish ties with Musavat Party, get necessary instructions
> recruit new members into the organization from
> nationalistic-minded youth irrespective of their social status
> and party affiliation; canvass nationalistic ideas
> among students of Baku and, if possible among students
> from other part of Azerbaijan. (CSA file 27, sh. 175)

The leaders of the organization intended to issue an illegal wall newspaper for members of the organization, using for this purpose a shapirograph of Komsomol collective under Baku Pedagogical College. They thought it was not a difficult task to tackle with, since one of them—Gasim Aslanov—headed a propaganda section of the students collective forum. Organizers established a membership fee of 50 copecks per year to receive Musavat literature and help poor members.

Responsibilities of the leading 'three' were distributed as follows:

Hassan Aqa Akhundzadeh—Executive Secretary; Gasim Aslanov—Head of organizational department; Ali Aqa Aslanov—treasurer. According to the decisions to be adopted by the 'three', each member of the organization was to head a new 'three'. Each new member, in turn, should have organized a new 'three' and so on. Thus, the organization was based on cells of three persons headed by the leading 'three'. This was accounted for by secrecy of actions and the leading 'three's' desire to protect a greater part of the organization from repressions by punitive organs in case of failure of some members.

After the situation around organizational matters became clear, the leading 'three' got down to implementing targeted goals and tasks. It was initially planned to create cells in three educational centres where the organizers maintained contacts with their accomplices—the Baku Pedagogical College under the People's Commissariat for Education; the pedagogical college under the Baku branch of Public Education; and working faculty under the Lenin Factory. Each member of the leading 'three' nominated a candidature to draw into the organization.

With the start of the 1927-8 academic year, the organizers got down to the implementation of the programme. First, they established contacts with Musavat through members of the illegal Kala-Mashtaga branch. Second, they started recruiting new members among the pupils, followed by obligatory talks on national matter. Soon after, the organization was widened through involvement of additional 12 members of Ganj Azer, both pupils and teachers, well aware of the purposes and tasks of the organization. Note that Ganj Azer maintained regular contacts with Musavat through members of the illegal branches of the party in Azerbaijan, received printed matter issued in Turkey, including such famous magazines as *Yeni Kavkaziye* (New Caucasus) and *Azeri-Turk*. Members of the leading 'three' expanded their activities in 1928 through establishing ties with students from the town of Kuba (CSA file 27, sh. 178).

The main part of the work of the organization was propaganda of nationalistic ideas, anti-Soviet propaganda among Azerbaijani youth, and distribution of literature. Contributing to the young students were librarians of Baku who, as members of Musavat, secretly received materials and literature of nationalistic nature, largely from Turkey.

As a consequence of Ganj Azer activities, some members of the organization, under the influence of the propaganda, decided to go to Turkey to proceed with their education abroad. Their elder comrades-in-arms undertook to help them through holding preliminary talks with Turkish consulate officials in Baku. However, before long, the activities of Ganj Azer came into the open by punitive bodies of Azerbaijan. In January 1929, ASPD summed up information provided by its intelligence network in educational institutions of Baku and began mass arrests of students. Using various methods of pressuring the people under investigation, the Soviet state apparatus succeeded in disclosing members of other cells, as well as Musavat Party members related to Ganj Azer. During the investigation, thirty-seven persons were arrested. As follows from ASPD special report, nineteen were pupils of pedagogical colleges; seven teachers; three students of various higher educational institutions; and eight employees. Of them, thirteen were members of the Young Communist League, two were member of the Communist Party of Azerbaijan, and four were women. As for their social status, 'they came mostly from high ranking peasantry and intelligentsia, and one student was a worker' (CSA file 27, sh. 177).

Among the arrested there were leading members of the organization—Hassan Aqa Akhundzadeh, Gasim Aslanov, Ali Aqa Aslanov; rank-and-file members—Mamed Hussain Mehzadeh, Ali Muhtar Mehdizadeh, Mamed Zeynalov, as well as their tutors—Mesih Akhundzadeh, Mamed Ali Akhundzadeh, Abbas Ali Akhundzadeh.

Thus Ganj Azer had been operating for slightly above three years, and succeeded in implementing the initial plans of its programme. As an ASPD document indicated 'a leading kernel of the organization was liquidated, while Ganj Azer's actual activity proceeded on a larger scale . . .' (CSA file 27, sh. 166, 179).

More detailed consideration of the posts of the arrested members of the organization is indicative that names of those privy to the organization, including cells in the environs of Baku and other towns of the Republic, were not uncovered during the investigation. Investigation of the case of Ganj Azer organization lasted just three and a half months and punitive methods applied by Azerbaijan GPU.

Wearisome, incessant interrogators, confrontations, tortures and compulsions were part of interrogation. Document on 969 arrests indicate that main participants of the organization were young students of the pedagogical college (except for Hassan Aqa Akhundzadeh). They acknowledged their 'guilt', especially plans to establish an organization of 'nationalistic nature', reading of Musavat publications, etc., which, to a degree, eased their fate. A part of young participants, who admitted all their faults, including female detainees, were not condemned and got off with fear to last all their life. One of Ganj Azer organizers Gasim Aslanov, a 20-years old student of the Baku Pedagogical College, son of a peasant, and member of the Joint Communist League charged with Article 66 of the Criminal Code of the Azerbaijan SSR, was released. However, more experienced members of the organization, who denied all the accusations and pleaded not guilty, failed to escape severe punishment. It is significant that investigating bodies were first prone to accuse adults only, including teachers, students, librarians, etc., i.e. the so-called tutors of the young people. Therefore, despite the lack of direct proof of guilt, all the adults, including teacher Lakariya Mirzazadeh (46 years old), student, Abbas Ali Akhundzadeh (25 years old), student and head of the library Mamed Zeynalov (25 years old), were sentenced to three years imprisonment. The initiator of Ganj Azer Hassan Aqa Akhundzadeh was also sentenced to three years of imprisonment, 23-year old student Mamed Amin Muradov to two years (MNS sh. 178).

Of particular interest are other documents as well, especially those relating to Mamed Zeynalov. He denied his guilt and actively opposed the methods of investigation and went on a hunger-strike. His letters and appeals to the procurator's office of Azerbaijan are the illustrative of the inhuman tortures that drove to him to 'madness' (MNS sh. 200). Zeynalov was accused of carrying on anti-Soviet propaganda, organizing illegal work among the youth, ties with Musavat, and reading and spreading of anti-Soviet literature. As head of the Library of Miners' Association in Black Town, he received forbidden literature from Turkey and gave it to students, including members of Ganj Azer (MNS sh. 204). Zeynalov reaffirmed that 'as a worker of the cultural front and an ordinary librarian' he brought 'books to masses, workshops and factories', that 'he showed interest in raising the cultural level of the proletarian masses—workers' (MNS sh. 199). The style and spirit of these explanatory notes are indicative of the fact that the accused was well versed in ideological and propaganda guidelines of the time. He compared 'harmless' scientific, sporting magazines of Turkey with similar editions of the Soviet Union, but denied spreading of Musavat magazines, especially *Yeni Kavkaziye* (New Caucasus). It is obvious that the investigating bodies did not believe him, and subjected him to torture:

> Due to various tortures, applied by investigators Jabbarov, Vasin and Kuliyev, I was driven to madness . . . I was ill, suffered neurasthenia, aggravated by tuberculosis, emaciation, frequently fainted. . . . (MNS sh. 202)

Neither denial of his guilt, nor intercessions of his parents helped ease this man's fate. Even worse, he was charged with 'being a participant of another, yet unestablished grouping of anti-Soviet trend', quoting that among friends of Zeynalov there were people, condemned for their political views and exiled to Solovetsk camps, and even executed (MNS sh. 204).

Zeynalov shared the fate of his friends, and spent all three years of his imprisonment at the corrective-labour colony at Solovetsk camps on the northern territory of Soviet Russia, notable for its inclement climate and cruel camp conditions. According to documents, Zeynalov could not 'work at the camp' and by the time of his release in January 1932 he was 'in the team of convalescents' (MNS sh. 185).

It may be supposed that further fate of Ganj Azer was typical of tragic period of Stalin repressions and they failed 'to become valorous builders of socialism in Soviet Azerbaijan'. It is the fate of one person only, whose name had frequently been mentioned by the arrested, who might be considered a lucky exception—two members of the leading 'three' referred to pupil Nigar Rafibekova who conveyed them books, issued in Turkey, and maintained close contacts with the well-known man of letters and teacher Amin Abid (arrested and shot in 1937), etc. (CSA, file. 27, sh. 169).

The above-mentioned Nigar Rafibekova was a daughter of the well-known physician and governor of Ganjeh during the national government and shot by the Bolsheviks. She was 15-16 years old when Ganj Azer started in Azerbaijan. Her brother lived in Turkey, with whom she was in open correspondence. For some reasons, she was lucky to avoid arrest and punishment on the part of authorities. Later on, she became a people's poet of Azerbaijan.

It is well-known that Rafibekova and her husband, the famous Azerbaijanian poet Rasul Reza, who held top positions in literary and other state organizations, had always been under surveillance for their free-thinking and nationalism. According to the son of these prominent figures, well-known Azerbaijan writer and publicist Anar, his mother Nigar Rafibeily had never mentioned her involvement in Ganj Azer activity, perhaps, in an attempt to guard her children against unnecessary information during the Soviet times.

Ganj Azer failed to shape as a powerful and properly organized 'young movement' and acted as a supporter of the Musavat Party in Azerbaijan. One can fairly assert that there were no objective reasons for the organization to establish itself. The point is that the mechanism of the creation and consolidation of totalitarian regime in the Soviet Union was picking up strength and nullified all attempts to withstand this process.

REFERENCES

Archives of the Ministry of National Security of Azerbaijan (MNS), file PC-15805.

Central State Archives of Political Parties and Social Movements of the Azerbaijan Republic (CSA), fund 1, inventory 231.

Wimbush, S.E. *Divided Azerbaijan: Nation Building, Assimilation and Mobilization between Three States* (Soviet Asian Ethnic Frontiers, 1979).

CHAPTER 9

The 'Young Modernists' *vs.* the 'Old Turbans': Reform and Resistance in Pre-Colonial Morocco

FATIMA HARRAK

The influence of the Young Turks movement in Tunisia and Algeria, former Ottoman territories, is manifest in the eminent role played by the Young Tunisians (Ziyadeh 1962; Khairallah 1934) and Young Algerians (Ageron 1968; Laroui 1975: 130-8) in the genesis of the nationalist and reformist trends in these two north African countries. Although Morocco was never a part of the Ottoman Empire, its elite was inspired and stimulated by the ideals of pan-Islamism, constitutionalism, and progress advocated by a multitude of currents from the Middle East, in particular the 'Young' and the 'Salafiyya' movements which advocated respectively progress (*taraqqi*) and renaissance (*nahda*). The underlying principles and aspirations of these groups were disseminated within Morocco via various agents and channels—the printing press, correspondence between scholars, and first hand contact by Moroccan officials, scholars, students, pilgrims and businessmen, whether in Morocco, in Middle Eastern countries, in neighbouring Algeria and Tunisia or in Europe—and Paris in particular—where all these movements had a representation.

Evidence of the ideological influence of the 'Young' and Salafiyya movements is manifest in the literature and various reform attempts by the Moroccan government and the political elite in the first decade of the twentieth century. In fact, this elite used the language and terminology of these movements in its justification of the destitution of Sultan 'A. al-'Aziz (1894-1908) and investiture of Sultan 'A. Hafidh (1908-12) in 1907—an event known in Moroccan history as the 'Hafidhian revolution'.[1] Reference to the concepts of nationalism (the concept of *sha'b* is added to the Islamic concept of *umma*), pan-Islamism, freedom (*hurriyya*), despotism (*istibdad*), colonialism (*isti'mar*), liberation (*istiqlal*), spread of modern education (*al-'ulum al-waqtiyya*), etc., can be found in the literature and documents produced during the first decade of the twentieth century, and in particular in the three draft constitutions elaborated between 1907 and 1908.[2] Nonetheless, Morocco did not produce its 'Young Moroccans' movement, even if a local section of the 'Young Maghrib' youth group is believed to have been created in 1908 on the occasion of the brief passage of the Turkish military mission in Morocco (Burke III 1976: 132, 142, 221; Laroui 1977: 380-1).

Modes and Agents of Transmission of the New Ideas

1. *The Salafiyyas*

The eminent bibliographer and historian Muhammad al-Manuni (1985) revealed a mine of documents and texts testifying to the close relationship between the Moroccan *'ulama* and *Makhzan* (Moroccan government) officials on the one hand and the founders of the Salafiyya—Jamal al-Din al-Afghani (1839-97), Muhammad Abduh (1849-1905) and Rashid Rida (1865-1935)—on the other. Some of these texts are reproduced in the said book and many more are to be sought in the archives and private libraries. The abundant instances where the revue *Majallat al-Manar* (the lighthouse) of Rashid Rida reported on Moroccan events are further evidence of the close ties between the Egyptian intellectual elite and the scholars and decision-makers in Morocco. The Egyptian leaders of the Salafiyya movement encouraged the Moroccan Sultan, state officials and the religious elite to introduce the necessary reforms that would lead to the rebirth and renaissance (*nahda*) of Morocco, direct its march towards progress while preventing it from falling into the trap of foreign occupation.

MUHAMMAD AL-QABBAJ

Muhammad al-Qabbaj al-Fasi, a Moroccan businessman in residence in Egypt, was among the mediators of the Salafiyya in

Morocco, at the turn of the twentieth century (al-Manuni 1985: 300-3). Al-Qabbaj was a Moroccan tradesman who had travelled widely in the Middle East and settled in Egypt for a long time. According to the Moroccan Minister and scholar Muhammad b. al-Hasan al-Hajwi (1874-1956), al-Qabbaj was an assiduous student of Jamal al-Din al-Afghani. He used to attend his night classes, together with Muhammad 'Abduh, Sa'd Zaghlul (1857-1927) and other Egyptian reformist leaders (al-Hajwi: 38). For this reason he is considered to be the Moroccan link in the chain of transmission of the Salafiyya ideals taught by al-Afghani and Abduh.

MUHAMMAD B. 'A. AL-KABIR AL-KATTANI

The '*alim,* Sufi and Sharif Muhammad b. 'A. al-Kabir al-Kattani (d. 1909) was the uncontested leader of the Hafidhiyya revolution.[3] His close relations with the founders of the Salafiyya are unchallenged, but as a political activist al-Kattani did not refrain from flirting with other contemporary reformist trends.

Muhammad b. 'A. al-Kabir al-Kattani was a brilliant 'alim and the shaykh of the Kattaniyya Darqawiyya Sufi order. He is qualified by his biographers as an *'alim 'amil* (an engaged scholar), a *faqih* (jurist), a *muhaddith* (traditionist) and a brilliant public speaker. His main *zawiya* in Fez used to be a sort of salon where the latest academic works in the Muslim world were discussed. He considered himself to be a member of the *Ahl al-Hadith* network and maintained regular correspondence with his fellows from West Africa to Hyderabad or Delhi. Al-Kattani was also a Sufi shaykh, and as such he had numerous adepts disseminated in the *tariqa* lodges which were spread out in the cities as in the countryside, in Arab—as well as in Berber-speaking country (al-Kattani 1962).

Muhammad b. 'A. al-Kabir al-Kattani was the recognized leader, ideologue and activist of the Hafidiyya revolution of 1907.[4] Like Muhammad Abduh he promoted Islamic religious reform and, following the example of Jamal al-Din al-Afghani, he advocated pan-Islamism and the unity of the *ummah.* He called for defensive *jihad* and pronounced himself strongly against the system of foreign protection. This, however, did not mean that he rejected Western culture altogether. On the contrary, he often urged his contemporaries to adopt the worthy values that made Europe powerful, and among these the value of 'freedom' (*al-hurriyya*) which he translated in the language of the *shari'a* as 'justice, equity, sincere admonition and a sense of responsibility.' When in 1907 he was asked by his colleagues to expose the conditions attached to the *bay'a* (allegiance) of the newly invested sultan, A. al-Hafidh, he listed , among other things, the following clauses:

- The establishment of an consultative assembly (*majlis al-shura*)
- The setting up of a strategic alliance with Muslim countries, and with Turkey in particular
- Reliance on Turkish military expertise to build Morocco's military capacity
- The banning of the clientalist and patronage system and the nomination of the right persons in the right positions
- The actualization of education to include mathematics and the various applied sciences.[5]

MUHAMMAD B. JA'FAR AL-KATTANI (d. 1929)

He belonged to the same Sharifian, Sufi and scholarly Kattani family. Like his cousin, he was also an eminent jurist and traditionist. His sense of mission took him to Syria and Hijaz where he taught and propagated the ideas of the Salafiyya. His *Nasihat ahl al-Islam* (Advice to Muslims) (M. al-Kattani 1908) became a reference work for later anti-colonialist and nationalist leaders. In this admonition addressed to all Muslims, Muhammad b. Ja'far al-Kattani identifies eleven causes for the debacle of the Muslim world:

- Division of the *ummah*
- Neglect of the development of military capacity
- Abandonment of *jihad*
- Irresponsible leadership
- Alliance with the *kuffar* (non-believers)
- Imitation of foreign manners without discernment
- Injustice and oppression
- Abandonment of the teaching of the Koran and Sunna

- Open practice of the illicit
- Predilection for material well-being
- Abandonment of *Nasiha/Shura*, i.e. consultation.[6]

Obviously, to these eleven erring and transgressions there are corresponding eleven reparations or antidotes, among which the promotion of unity and solidarity of the Muslim community, the development of its military capacity, the revitalization of *jihad*, the revivication of the institution of *shura*, the advancement of justice and equity and compliance with the teachings of the Koran and the Sunna.

This epistle was widely read by the author's contemporaries, but also by later Moroccan nationalists, including Muhammad b. 'A. al-Karim al-Khattabi, the champion of the Rif resistance, who considered this epistle as his 'guide' in his *jihad* against Spanish occupation (Laroui 1977: 391).

2. *Progress (al-Taraqqi)*

Al-Qabbaj, Muhammad b. 'A. al-Kabir al-Kattani and Muhammad b. Ja'far al-Kattani would have probably liked to identify themselves as Salafis and as followers in the footsteps of Al-Afghani and Muhammad Abduh. We must not forget that, in the early twentieth century the Salafiyya was a 'renaissance' (*nahda*) movement led by an enlightened and progressive Muslim intellectual elite. So, we should not be surprised by the similarity of their petitions with those of their more 'modern' contemporaries.

The modernists came from different horizons but they evolved in a traditional society where the language of the *shari'a* was the common denominator among the various political forces. Who were this young 'modernists'?

MOROCCAN STUDENTS IN EUROPE

Since the end of the nineteenth century Moroccan students were sent to Europe to acquire scientific knowledge (Laroui 1977: 282-9).[7] These students came in contact with the ideas of modernity as lived by Europeans and as advocated by the 'Young Turks' groups present in Europe. Among these several names are recurrent in the history of Morocco during this first decade of the twentieth century:

- Al-Zubayr Skiredj
- Ahmad al-Jabli
- Al-Tahar b. al-Haj Loudiyyi, and
- Al-Tayyib Mustapha al-Zawali Tanji (Al-Manuni 1985: I 254-6, 284, II 308)

These young men who mastered several foreign languages acted as translators and interpreters during the negotiations with European powers. They also read the foreign press and reported its content to the local and aging *ulama* who were the veritable leaders of the constitutionalist and anti-colonialist movement during this era.

MOROCCANS WHO LIVED IN THE MASHRIQ

The other Moroccan group who came in contact with the ideas of modernity and progress were the Moroccan businessmen who travelled extensively in the Mashriq or lived for a long time in one or many of the Middle Eastern countries. They had a first hand experience of all the intellectual and political currents in vogue at the time. While in the Mashriq, they served as guides to other Moroccans who visited the area on their pilgrimage journey, and when they returned home they were the depositories of the new ideals. I have already presented al-Haj al-Qabbaj, the student of al-Afghani. 'Ali Zniber al-Salawi (d. 1914) who returned to Morocco from Egypt in 1905 is another major agent of ideas of progress and *taraqqi* in Morocco. He is the author of a memorandum to Sultan 'A. al-'Aziz and of the first draft constitution for Morocco (al-Manuni 1985: II 399-401).

Another Moroccan who was brought up in Tunisia is 'Abd al-Hakim al-Mazughi al-Tunusi. This young man spoke Turkish and mastered several other European languages. He was recruited into the Moroccan Foreign Service which he served in Tangiers, France and Turkey. He was considered by the leaders of the nationalist movement who resorted to his council as an expert on international affairs (al-Manuni: 1985: II 312, 322-6).

TUNISIAN, EGYPTIAN, SYRIAN, LEBANESE AND TURKISH IMMIGRANTS AND VISITORS

Of foremost importance was the impact of the Arab and Muslim press which found its way to Morocco during the last decade of the nineteenth century. The number of newspapers and periodicals that reached Morocco through the European postal services in Tangier was certainly limited but it was fully exploited through the reading clubs that emerged in the cities. Among the numerous titles which reached Fez, for example, we should mention *Thamarat al-funun* (the fruit of arts) from Damascus, *al-Ma'lumat* (informations) from Istanbul, *Bayrut* from Lebanon and many more titles from Egypt such as *al-Manar* (the lighthouse), *al-Mu'ayyad* (the supported) and *Al Liwa'* (the flag) (Lahrishi 2003: 116).

The ideas and ideals of modernity were also defended by visitors and immigrants who settled in Morocco. Among the most eminent visitors in this early twentieth century is the Tunisian 'Alim Muhammad Khayr Eddine (d. 1889). He remained in Marrakech for two years as a guest of the Moroccan government during which period he met with the Moroccan *ulama*, including Shaykh Muhammad b. 'A. al-Kabir al-Kattani (Lahrishi 2003: 309-10).

The Egyptian journalist 'Ali Zaki who came to Morocco to cover the Algesiras Conference for the newspaper *al-Mu'ayyid* is reported to have acted as an advisor to the Moroccan delegation at the said conference.[8] His services were so prized that he was recruited into the *Makhzan* (Moroccan central government). He filled the positions of the Director of Public Works and officer at the Ministry of Agriculture. 'Alizaki' died in Morocco in 1929 (Lahrishi 2003: 310-11; A. al-Kattani n.d.).

The Syrian 'Alim 'Abd al-Karim b. 'Umar b. Mustapha b. al-Shaykh Murad came to Fez also in 1906-7. He was received at the Kattani Zawiya in Fez where he started teaching Geography, Koran recitation, Astronomy, Mathematics and History. He counted among his students a number of later leaders of the Moroccan nationalist movement, such as the judge 'A. al-Hafidh al-Fasi (uncle of Allal al-Fasi).

During his stay in Morocco 'A. al-Karim Murad wrote a memorandum to Sultan 'A. al-'Aziz recommending the creation of a modern primary school where the children will be taught the religious and modern (*al-waqtiyya*/contemporary) sciences; this school was to be called '*al-maqasid al-'aziziyya li-nashr al-'ulum al-diniyya wa al-waqtiyya*' (the intentions of 'Abd al-'Aziz to spread the religious and contemporary sciences) (al-Manuni 1985). 'Abd al-Karim Murad also wrote a draft constitution in 1907 which neither Allal al-Fasi nor 'Abd Allah Laroui could identify, it was Muhammad al-Manuni in the early 1980s who found a copy of this constitution signed by the author.[9]

The list of immigrants from the Middle East who settled in Morocco in the early twentieth century would not be complete without reference to the Lebanese community of Tangiers. Two Christian Lebanese families played a major role in the promotion of progressive ideas in Morocco through the establishment of an Arabic Moroccan Press through the diffusion of books and newspapers from the Middle East and through the animation of a sort of club or intellectual salon. Michael Karam owned a renowned bookstore in Tangiers and his brother Wadi' Karam started a daily newspaper and a revue, *al-Sabah* (The Morning). Farah Allah Nemour started and directed the first official Moroccan newspaper, *Lisan al-Maghrib* (The Voice of the Maghrib), and his brother Arthur Nemour served as its chief editor. *Lisan al-Maghrib* was not just a newspaper, it was the focus of a circle of young Moroccan intellectuals and enlightened *ulama* of Fez, and a forum for expressing their ideas and ideals for a progressive and independent Morocco. It was the group of *Lisan al-Maghrib* who elaborated the 1908 draft constitution and it was on its column that this document was presented and addressed to Sultan 'A. al-Hafidh for the first time (al-Manuni 1985: 314-15).

All this does not tell us about the existence of a 'Young Moroccans' movement at this stage of Moroccan resistance to foreign encroachment. Both Allal al-Fasi in his *al-Harakat al-Istiqlaliya* and al-Manuni in an interview with Allal al-Fasi's uncle[10] acknowledge the fact that a secret society by the name of *Jam'iyyat al-Taraqqi* (Association of Progress) was formed in 1908 in Fez and assembled young Moroccans such as:

- 'A. al-Hafidh al-Fasi
- Muhammad b. 'A. al-Hayy al-Kattani
- 'Abbas al-Kardudi
- Al-Mahdi b. al-Talib al-Fasi
- 'A. al-'Aziz Lahlou
- Hassan Sqalli
- Ahmad al-Zabdi al-Ribati (al-Fasi 1948)

Members of this association, according to Allal al-Fasi, promoted the ideas of reform and progress in the articles they wrote for newspapers and in the meetings which they animated in various cities and towns.[11] This information, however, has never been confirmed by another source. In any case, the name of the association together with the fact that its creation coincided with the brief passage of the Turkish military mission in Fez, (Burke 1976: 142) may be misleading as to the ideological colour of the organization. A group of Ottoman military instructors were indeed sent by the Khedive of Egypt on the request of Sultan 'Abd al-Hafidh in 1908 but its stay in Morocco was curtailed under the pressure of France. Later on, one of the Turkish officers who made the journey, wrote a memorandum justifying his acceptance of the Moroccan mission. Pan-Islamism, he wrote, was a very popular idea at the time, but there was 'another more important factor which made us accept (the sultan's terms for recruitment), and that was our eagerness to show this country the way to civilized life and introduce it to Turkish culture' (Deny 1928: 221). That these Turkish officers had a sense of mission is understandable, but that they had the time to organize the Moroccan elite into a 'Young' movement has yet to be proved.

So the question remains: why didn't Morocco produce a 'Young' movement like its Arab and Muslim neighbours and contemporaries? And why did the leadership of the reformist and the nationalist movements in Morocco remain in the hands of the traditional *ulama*? I am tempted to reply that Morocco did not need a 'young Moroccans' movement, since the traditional religious elite was doing such a good job of adopting and adapting the ideas and ideals of 'modernity' and 'progress' to a highly traditional Moroccan reality.

The Hafidhian Revolution or the Triumph of the *Shari'a* Discourse

The Hafidhian revolution which led to the destitution of Sultan 'Abd al-'Aziz and the enthronement of his brother 'Abd al-Hafidh in 1907, is in many ways comparable to its contemporary Persian (1906) and Turkish (1908) revolutions, at least as far as the form is concerned. This was not a palace revolution. Two parties—the Hafidhite and the Azizite—confronted each other in a hot political and ideological debate which lasted for a decade and which prompted the development of a Moroccan Arabic press, the elaboration of a proto-nationalist thought and the emergence of a new political elite. The debate concerned the defence of the country against foreign occupation, in particular through the means of reform of the political system in the sense of a constitutional monarchy.

1. *The Constitutionalist Reform*

Opposition to foreign occupation, the promotion of pan-Islamism and constitutional reform of the State were the top requirements of the movement. Attempts to determine the source of inspiration for these ideas may look unproductive as contacts between the young Moroccans and their counterparts in the Arab Middle East were never interrupted. Whether they met during pilgrimage in the Holy land, study journeys, business trips or military missions in Paris, Damascus, Cairo or Rabat, the young Muslims and non-Muslim Arabic speakers of the region were facing the same challenges and were bound to exchange their views and learn from one another. How these same ideas of Islamic solidarity, Arab nationalism and constitutionalism were applied locally is what distinguished each specific movement.

The attempt by Moroccan elite to limit the powers of the sultan through the revival of the Islamic institution of *shura* (consultation, concretized in various forms of consultative bodies) and the creation of a consultative assembly was already attempted under Sultan Mawlay al-Hassan in 1860 (Laroui 1977: 228-30). The early twentieth-century constitutionalist movement expressed itself in two ways: the petition for a consultative assembly in 1904 and the submission of three draft constitutions between 1906 and 1908.

PETITION FOR A CONSULTATIVE ASSEMBLY

When in April 1904 France and England signed an 'entente' by which Britain traded her claims for Morocco for France's readiness to abandon her 'rights' over Egypt, Sultan 'Abd al-'Aziz and his entourage realized that it was the end of Morocco's independence. It was at this occasion that the *ulama*, the urban political elite and some progressive members of the *Makhzan* renewed the call for a consultative assembly (*Majlis al-A'yan*). The memorandum that Sultan 'Abd al-'Aziz addressed in December 1904 to the governors of the Moroccan provinces aimed at the formation of a veritable representative national assembly:

> It is our duty to discuss unprecedented events which jeopardize our future as a community. Our subjects must elect among the notables of each tribe the most honest and sensible persons whom they are ready to trust with the defense of their faith, their honor and their wealth. These deputies (*nuwwab*) are called upon to help us find solutions to the problems that we are facing. Consultation will thus be general and the result can only be to the benefit of all, as God has promised us. As soon as you receive this memorandum, assemble and elect your deputies. (Laroui 1977: 377)

The *Majlis* was not, and could not be, an inefficient arm against French colonial plans. What it did, however, was to allow Sultan 'Abd al-'Aziz to assemble and consult the elite and discuss with them the French reforms advocated by the French minister Taillandier in 1904 (Burke 1976: 80-5). By so doing, the sultan demonstrated his goodwill to both the French minister and the Moroccan elite. These latter were only too happy to take part in the work of the *Majlis* because they believed that democratic reform was not only a course of resisting colonialism but also a means of curbing despotism.

ZNIBER'S MEMORANDUM AND DRAFT CONSTITUTION

It was in this same perspective that in 1906 a memorandum was sent to Sultan 'Abd al-'Aziz by a member of the political elite, al-

Haj 'Ali b. Ahmad Zniber al-Salawi (d. 1914), proposing a draft constitution for Morocco (al-Manuni 1985: II 408-15).[12]

Who is 'Ali Zniber? Born around 1844, he emigrated with his parents to the Holy lands where his parents died. He returned to Sale where he probably had his education. We find him exercising trade in Fez, then in Alexandria and Tanta. He was among the people that the Moroccan 'alim and political activist 'Abd al-Hayy al-Kattani met during his pilgrimage journey in 1903-4. After 23 years in Egypt, 'Ali Zniber returned to Morocco in 1904 where he witnessed the French reform proposals of the Minister Taillandier and the Algesiras conference in 1906. In addition to the draft constitution which he entitled 'Preserving Independence and Rejecting Occupation' (*hifz al-istiqlal wa lafz al-ihtilal*), Ali Zniber left numerous poems, letters and a critical analysis of the Algesiras treaty.[13]

There is no doubt as to the source of inspiration of 'Ali Zniber. What interests us though is how he adapted all the ideas and ideals with which he was familiar in Egypt to the Moroccan reality?

The author divides his memorandum into three parts:

- Definition of the concept of *Istiqlal* (independence)
- Definition of the concept of *Ihtilal* (occupation)
- List of proposed reforms.[14]

'Independence', according to 'Ali Zniber, describes the juridical status of the 'state of Morocco' (*dawlat murrakush*) as recognized by the Algesiras Conference. 'The Kingdom of Morocco' (*mamlakat al-maghrib al-aqsa*) is independent both internally and externally and its sovereignty is exercised on its land and on its seas. In order to consolidate this independence, Zniber calls the attention of Sultan 'Abd al-'Aziz to the necessity of forming a committee of notables composed of the nation's most enlightened minds. All the constituting elements of the nation (*jami' afrad al-wataniyya*) will contribute to the selection of this committee. They will delegate it to represent them in examining the reforms proposed by the Algesiras Conference. The Sultan, as head of the executive, will see to it that the evaluation and opinion of these delegates, who are the nation's free-thinkers and men of thought and action (*ahrar al-umma wa arbab al-fikr wa al-qariha*), are confirmed and implemented.

The author then goes on to define *al-ihtilal*, showing the parallel between despotism, which he calls 'national occupation' (*al-ihtilal al-watani*), and foreign occupation (*al-ihtilal al-ajnabi*). This leads him to the conclusion that the best way to avoid foreign occupation is to stay vigilant and avoid all the traps that pave the way for foreign aggression. This starts by making some strategic choices: putting forward freedom against absolutism and opting for the way of progress against stagnation.

Zniber then goes on to the third part of the memorandum which lists the proposed reforms. These touch several domains:

- The system of representation: it must rely on an elected assembly of the enlightened minds of the country, headed by the best among them, who work for reforming the country.
- The system of government: it is based on a monarchy which acts in sovereignty and independence from any foreign pressure, deals justly with all its subjects, acts firmly against unjust governors or traitors and applies all the reforms recommended to it by the deputies of the *umma*.
- The objectives of the nation: unity and equality of all nationals, without distinction, before the laws of the land, civil peace and security, promotion of Arabic as the official language of the Kingdom, recruitment of competent personnel into the *Makhzan* apparatus, progress through reform, introduction of modern education, economic and financial independence.
- Morocco's foreign relations: they must be based on reciprocity. The interests of all foreign nations in Morocco are protected as long as these respect the interests of Moroccan government and people (al-Manuni 1985: II 408-21).

MURAD'S DRAFT CONSTITUTION

Around the same time, and as the Hafidhian revolution was gaining momentum, another memorandum and draft constitution were presented to Sultan 'A. al-'Aziz. This time the author was not a Moroccan, but a Syrian 'alim and friend of Shaykh Muhammad

b. 'A. al-Kabir al-Kattani, Abd al-Karim Murad al-Tarabulsi al-Madani (d. 1928).

We have seen that the Syrian *'alim* 'A. al-Karim Murad who arrived in Morocco in 1906 was the guest of Shaykh Muhammad b. 'A. al-Kabir al-Kattani in Fez, and taught Geography, Astromony, Mathematics and History at the Zawiya Kattaniyya, and wrote a memorandum to the sultan recommending the establishment of a school that teaches 'religious and modern sciences'. His draft constitution, however, has and remains till today one of the most read and commented documents of Moroccan contemporary history. It is because, somehow, this Syrian *alim* was able to mirror in this text the paradox of what would become the Moroccan nationalist movement: a traditionalist association dressed up in modern clothes.

'A. al-Karim Murad's memo to Sultan 'A. al-'Aziz is divided in four parts: a preamble, a section dedicated to national representation, a part relative to the reform of the military and a fourth part concerned with the financial organization.[15]

In the preamble the author asserts having found in Morocco the basic ingredients that are at the root of every progress (*asl kull taraqqi*) and which allowed Japan to resist the hegemony of its neighbours and become a world power: national unity (*ittihad al-jins*), attachment to religion and love for the ruling king. The author then stresses the necessity for Morocco to develop a fundamental law which would govern social relations. As this has been done in Persia, a Muslim country, this law should be based on the opinion of the Mujtahids of the Maliki school of jurisprudence predominant in Morocco. 'A. al-Karim Murad upholds that, like the Persian Muslims, Moroccans are not opposed to reforms but are eager to see them neither contradict the *shari'a* nor lead to foreign occupation of their land.

The author then goes on to recommend the reforms that are necessary in order to face up to European challenges:

1. First on the list is the establishment of a national assembly, which he calls interchangeably *Majlis al-milla* or *Majlis al-umma* (national assembly) and defines in Shari'a terms

as *Majlis al-shura* (consultative assembly) decreed by the Prophet Muhammad. In 12 articles he suggests its composition, competence, functioning and role. At no time are we left to forget that this is an assembly of a Muslim nation: the deputies have a basic knowledge of *fiqh*, the laws and regulations promulgated by the house must conform to the *shari'a* (Islamic law), and all non-Koranic taxes must be abolished.

2. The second most important reform is that of the military. Here the author's expertise is limited. His proposals are simplistic: continue to use the European military experts for forming officers and use these officers to train the population. This implies the return to mass mobilization.
3. The third reform concerns the finances and state's management of its income. In this domain the author of this document remains attached to traditional institutions, the *zawaya* (religious orders) and the *waqf* (endowments) foundation.

Abdallah Laroui estimates that, at this point, 'A. al-Karim Murad simply reproduced the Egyptian reform of the religious endowments (Laroui 1975: 380). Thus, notwithstanding the use of modern concepts, such as despotism (*istibdad* and *hukm mutlaq*), European civilization (*tamaddun urubbawi*), patriotism (*hubb al-watan*), and the reference made to the example of Turkey, this project is essentially inspired from the more traditional Egyptian and Persian reforms. In all his recommendations to Sultan 'A. al-'Aziz the Syrian '*alim* remains conscious of the necessity that all the proposals he makes conform to Divine law of which he accepted as custodian and depository.

2. *Follow-up of the Hafidhian Revolution*

A few months after the investiture of the new Sultan 'A. al-Hafidh on the basis of a conditional *bay'a*, which is in itself a veritable constitutional charter, the newspaper and association *Lisan al-Maghrib*, which had its headquarters in Fez, wrote an editorial renewing the demand for a Constitution:

> His Majesty can no longer refuse to his people the benefits of a constitution and a parliament. His Majesty must guarantee to his people the freedom of expression and action which enable them to reform their country like the other Muslim and Christian nations. . . . We have just seen the happy changes introduced in the Ottoman Empire through the proposal by the Prince of Believers of a Constitution and His decision to assemble a Parliament. . . . May we rapidly follow this example.

In October-November 1908 the same newspaper published in four issues the text of a draft constitution.[16] The document is divided into chapters and the chapters into articles. So, the form is that of a standard European constitution.

The first chapter deals with the state, its nature, its independence, its capital, its religion, its king and his rights and duties.

The second chapter is dedicated to the citizen and his rights and obligations: civil liberty, work, freedom of expression, obligation of primary education, equality of citizens before the law, freedom of circulation, security of life and wealth, abolition of torture, beating, pillage, corvee and all illegal modes of punishment.

The third chapter organizes the prerogatives and work of the two chambers which form the Moroccan parliament (the National Assembly and the Assembly of the Sharifs). It also discusses the rights and obligations of the deputies and the parliamentarian immunity. The project also addresses the responsibilities of government, the state budget, the educational system and the revision of the constitution.

Conclusion

The 'Moroccan crisis' kindled by a succession struggle following the death of Mawlay al-Hasan in 1894 led to the breaking up of the traditional Moroccan political system based on the *bay'a* (allegiance) to a sultan commander of the faithful (*amir al-mu'minin*). The fourteen years old 'A. al-'Aziz was put and maintained on the throne not by the *bay'a* of *ahl al-hall wa al-'aqd* (people of tying and untying) but by the intrigues of European powers and their agents in the Court. There followed the isolation of the sultan, the appearance of independent *jihad* leaders in the countryside and in the threatened peripheries (Sahara, Shinguit and Rif) and the division of the *Makhzan* apparatus into partisans of reform imposed from outside by European powers, and the supporters of the re-actualization and revitalization of the traditional *bay'a* system. This restoration attempt was initiated by the Moroccan traditional religious elite (*ulama*, *shurafa* and Sufis), whose *shari'a* discourse was the only straightforward discourse available, and was backed by Muslim and Arab reformists of all tendencies. This effort was unsuccessful and Sultan 'A. al-Aziz yielded more and more to French demands. Short of rejecting the regime or the Alawi dynasty altogether, the Moroccan political forces chose to give another chance to the *bay'a* system in the person of Mawlay 'A. al-Hafidh.

The Hafidhian revolution impressed the discourse of the *shar'* which became the common language of the Moroccan society and the symbol of its unity. Indeed, from the very beginning European pressure imperiled the sultanat, the predominance of the *shari'a* and threatened the established social order. The *shar'* became the unique language in which the aspirations of all these social categories could be expressed.

NOTES

1. While al-Fasi (1948: 95) qualifies the destitution of Mawlay 'Abd al-'Aziz as a 'revolution', Laroui (1977: 371-2) prefers to identify the event as a 'Hafidian movement'.
2. Two draft constitutions were issued in 1906 and a third one in 1908. These texts were known to the Moroccan political activists at the time, as this is attested by the existence of several manuscript copies of the 1906 draft. As for the 1908 constitution, it was published in the nationalist weekly *Lisan al-Maghrib* in four issues between October and November 1908.
3. The role played by this 'alim and Sufi at different stages of the movement for the dethronement of Sultan 'Abd al-'Aziz are detailed in Laroui (1975: 373-96).
4. Abd al-Hafid Mawlay 'himself recognized his political power and authority when he addressed him as the 'most sublime shaykh and gnostic, the complete wali and sharif' (Letter dated 10 Rajab 1325/ 20 Aug. 1907, Archives Royales, Rabat, collection 'al-Tartib al-Khass').
5. See the text of the *Bay'a* of Fez to Sultan 'Abd al-Hafid in al-Manuni (1985: 349-53). For comments on this Bay'a see Tawfiq (1987: 335-47).

6. Exerpts from the *Nasihat* are found in al-Manuni (1985: 376-85).
7. Between 1885 and 1888, for example, 12 Moroccan students were sent to the School of Engineering at Montpelier in France where they studied the genie militaire, according to Jacques Caille (*Hesperis*, 31 (1954: 12). See also list of other students delegations in al-Manuni (1985: I, 167-87).
8. See the newspaper *As-Saada,* issue of 21 June 1906, BNR.
9. See the complete text of this draft constitution as well as a reproduction of the colophon of the manuscript copy in the author's handwriting in Al-Manuni (1985: II, 422-45).
10. Al-Manuni informs us that he had this interview with the judge 'A. al-Hafid al-Fasi in the latter's house in Rabat in 1955 (al-Manuni 1985: II, 309).
11. Allal al-Fasi quotes *Lisan al-Maghrib* which exposes the ideas of this association; see his al-Fasi 1948: 98-9).
12. The memorandum comes as an introduction to Zniber's draft constitution.
13. Among these there is a critical essay about the Algesiras Conference of 1906 (Ms. 557 in Bibilotheque Sbihiyya de Sale (BSS) and Microfilm # 520, BNR).
14. I rely for the presentation of this memoradum on the text found in Appendice 67 of al-Manuni (1985: 408-21).
15. I rely for the presentation of this text on al-Manuni (1985: 422-45).
16. This text is analysed notably by al-Fasi (1948: 99-101). A translation into French of the text of this constitution has been published by Cagne (1988: 1-7).

REFERENCES

Ageron, Ch. R., *Les mususlmans algériens et la France*, 2 vols. (Paris: PUF, 1968).

al-Kattani, Al-Baqir, *Tarjamat al-shaykh Muhammd al-Kattani al-Shahid* (Rabat: Imprimerie al-Fajr, 1962).

Burke III, Edmond, *Prelude to Protectorate in Morocco* (Chicago: University of Chicago Press, 1976).

Cagne, Jacques, 'Le projet de constitution d'un journal tangérois au début du siècle', *Revue Dar Al-Niaba*, no. 18 (1988).

Deny, Jean, 'Instructeurs militaires turcs au Maroc sous Moulay Hafidh', in *Mémorial Henri Basset* (Paris: Durand, 1928).

al-Fasi, Allal, *al-Harakat al-istiqlaliya fi al-maghrib al-'arabi* (Tangier: Abessalam Guassus, 1948).

al-Hajwi, Muhammad b. al-Hasan, *Al-'urwatu al-wuthqa,* Ms #H/140, Bibliotheque Nationale de Rabat (BNR), n.d.

al-Kattani, 'A. al-Hayy, *Mudhakkirat,* Ms. 13096, Bibliotheque Hassaniya de Rabat (BHR).

al-Kattani, Muhammad b. Ja'far, *Nasihat ahl al-Islam* (Advice to Muslims), (Fez: Lith., 1908).

Khairallah, Chedly, *Le mouvement évolutionniste tunisien* (Tunis: de Tunis, 1934).

Laroui, Abdallah, *L'histoire du Maghreb* (Paris: Maspero, 1975).

les origines sociales et culturelles du nationalisme Marocain (Paris: Maspero, 1977).

Lahrishi, Abd Al-Rahman, *Al Madrasa Al Nasiriya bi Fas* (Casablanca: Al Najah Al Jadida, 2003).

al-Manuni, Muhammad, *Mazahir yaqadhat al-maghrib al-hadith* (Apects of the awakening of modern North Africa), 2 vols. (Beirut: Dar al-Gharb al-Islami, 1985).

Tawfiq, Ahmad, 'Ta'ammulat fi al-Bay'a al-Hafidhiyya', in *Al-Maghrib mina al-'ashd al-'Azizi ila sanat 1912,* I (Mohammedia: Al-Jami'a al-Sayfiyya, 1987).

Ziyadeh, N., *Origins of Nationalisms in Tunisia* (Beirut: Catholique, 1962).

Contributors

SAMIM AKGÖNÜL is a historian and political scientist, and a researcher at the French National Center for Scientific Research and Associate Professor at the Marc Bloch University of Strasbourg. His area of research is Turkish political history, especially the minority issues in Turkey and the Balkans. He is the author of *Une communauté, deux Etats: la minorité turco-musulmane de Thrace occidentale* (Istanbul, 1999), *Les Grecs de Turquie: processus d'extinction d'une minorité de l'âge de l'Etat nation à l'âge de la mondialisation* (Leuven, 2004), *Le Patriarcat grec orthodoxe: de l'isolement à l'internationalisation* (Paris, 2005), *Religions de Turquie, religions des Turcs: nouveaux acteurs dans l'Europe élargie* (Paris, 2006), and *De la nomination en turc actuel: appartenances, perceptions, croyances* (Istanbul, 2007). His current research is on religious minorities.

DILOROM AGZAMOVNA ALIMOVA has been since 2000 Director of the Institute of History, Academy of Sciences of the Republic of Uzbekistan. She was the co-chairman of the organizing committee of the workshop 'Young Movements in the History of the South', October 2003 in Tashkent, of which the publication 'Modernity and its Agencies' is the result. She has published over 150 articles and books and among which *Women's Shape in Uzbekistan before and after Independence // Danger and Identity Construction Women of Central Asia, Caucuses and Turkey* (Brill London-Boston-Köln, 2000) in English; Editor of *Turkistan in the Beginning of 20th Century: On the Historical Roots of National Independence*, (Tashkent, 2000), in Russian; and *Essays on the History of Statehood*, (Tashkent, 2001), in Russian and Uzbek; *Uzbekistan in 1917-1991s: Confrontatin of Ideas and Ideologies* (Tashkent, 2002, co-author A. Golovanov) in Russian; *History of Tashkent (From the Ancient Times to the Present Days)* (Tashkent, 2007, co-author M. Filanovich) in Russian; *Makhmukhodja Bekhbudi and his Historical Views* (Tashkent, 1998, co-author D. Rashidova) in Russian and Uzbek; *History as History, History as Science: History and Historical Consciousness*, vol. I (Tashkent, 2008), in Russian; *History as History, History as Science: Phenomenon of Djadidism*, vol. 2 (Tashkent, 2008) in Russian.

TOURAJ ATABAKI is Professor of Social History of the Middle East and Central Asia at Leiden University, Netherlends and Senior Research Fellow at the International Institute of Social History. He is the author of *Azerbaijan: Ethnicity and the Struggle for Power in Iran* (London, 1993), *Beyond Essentialism: Who Writes Whose Past in the Middle East and Central Asia?* (Amsterdam, 2003), editor of *Post-Soviet Central Asia* (London, 1998), co-editor, with Erik Jan Zürcher, of *Men of Order, Authoritarian Modernisation in Turkey and Iran* (London, 2004) and co-editor, with Sanjyot Mehendale, of *Central Asia and the Caucasus: Transnationalism and Diaspora* (London and New York, 2005). And editor of *Iran and the First World War: A Battleground of the Great Powers* (London, 2006), *The State and the Subaltern: Society and Politics in Turkey and Iran* (London, 2007), *Iran in the Twentieth Century: Historiography and Political Culture* (London, 2009). His current work focuses on labour history of Iran and comparative historiography of Iran and Central Asia since the nineteenth century.

KAVEH BAYAT is an independent researcher working in Iran. He is the editor of the *Contemporary History of Iran* and *Central Asia and Caucasus* series in the Shirazeh Ketab Publishing Co. and hss published extensively in Persian on modern history, especially military and tribal politics.

ROSINKA CHAUDHURI is a Fellow in Cultural Studies at the Centre for Studies in Social Sciences, Calcutta. She is the author of *Gentlemen Poets in Colonial Bengal: Emergent Nationalism and the Orientalist Project* (Calcutta, 2002) and has contributed chapters to *An Illustrated History of Indian Literature in English* (Delhi, 2003) and *Interpreting Homes in South Asian Literature* (Delhi, 2007).

She has published widely, her articles appearing in *Interventions: An International Journal of Postcolonial Studies, Studies in History, Indian Economic and Historical Review, Economic and Political Weekly, Social Text,* and *Modern Asian Studies.* Her latest book is *Derozio, Poet of India: The Definitive Edition* (London, 2008). At the moment she is working on a book tentatively titled 'Poetry and Political Consciousness in Late Nineteenth-Century Bengal.'

NADIR DEVLET is Professor of Turkic social, political, cultural history and international relations. He has specialized on Turkic peoples of Russia, Caucasus and Central Asia. Among others he is the author of *Liderligin Efendisi Cengiz Han* [The Master of Leadership: Chingiz Khan] (İstanbul, 2007), *Yıraq koenchyshtagy Tatar-Bashqortlarga ni buldı?* [What Happened to Tatar-Bashkirs in the Far-east?] (Kazan, 2005) (in Tatar), *Studies in the Politics, History and Culture of Turkic Peoples* (Istanbul, 2005); *Empires in Eurasia from Chingiz Khan to 20th Century* (Istanbul, 2002); *Rusya Türklerinin Milli Mücadele Tarihi (1905-1917)* [National Struggle History of Russian Turks], 2nd edn. (Ankara, 1999); *1917 Ekim İhtilali ve Türk-Tatar Millet Meclisi* [1917 October Revolution and Turk-Tatar National Paliament] (Istanbul, 1998), *İdil-Ural Ekspedisyonu: Tatarlar-Başkurtlar-Çuvaşlar* [Volga-Ural Expedition: Tatars-Bashkirs-Chuvashs] (Ankara, 1997). He lectures and conducts research on international relations and security topics also. He is Foreign Relations Specialist at Strategic Research Center of General Staff.

FATIMA HARRAK is Research Professor in Intellectual and Religious History and former Director of the Institute of African Studies at University Mohammed V-Souissi in Rabat. She is author notably of *West African Pilgrims in Nineteenth Century Morocco* (Rabat, 1999) and author in collaboration of *Mi'raj al-Su'ud-Ahmad Baba's Replies on Slavery* (Rabat, 2000) and *A Fulani Jihadist in the Maghrib* (Rabat, 2000). She is coordinator of the Research Team 'Religious Dynamics in Africa', Member of the Scientific Committee of the Journal *Al-Maghrib al-Ifriqi* and Vice-President of the Council for the Development of Research in the Social Sciences in Africa (CODERIA). Her research interests cover Islamic religious reform movements, intellectual history and religious dynamic in Africa.

MANSURA HAIDAR, specialist on Central Asian history, has been associated with Aligarh Muslim University (India) where she worked as Dean, Faculty of Social Sciences, Coordinator of Centre of Advanced Study and Chairman, Department of History. Presently, she is a Visiting Professor at Jamia Millia Islamia, New Delhi. She is the author of several books and over hundred articles. Her recent publications include *Letters of Emperor Akbar* (New Delhi, 1998); *Central Asia in the Sixteenth Century* (New Delhi, 2002); *Central Asian Impact on Mughal Polity* (New Delhi, 2003); *Indo-Central Asian Relations* (New Delhi, 2003); *Medieval Central Asia* (New Delhi, 2004); co-editor with S.H. Bira of *India and Mongolia* (New Delhi, 1997); editor of *Sufis, Sultans and Feudal Lords* (New Delhi, 2004); her current work focuses on Indo-West and Central Asian Exchanges in the Sphere of Medical Sciences, Fine Arts and Technology.

SOLMAZ RUSTAMOVA-TOHIDI is Professor of History and Senior Research Fellow at the Institute of Oriental Studies of Azerbaijan Academy of Sciences. She is the author of *Emigre Press of the Iranian Communist Party, 1917–1932* (Persian language) (Baku, 1985); *The Azerbaijan Periodic Press* (Baku, 1993); *Baku Documents: Union Catalogue of Persian, Azerbaijani, Ottoman Turkish and Arabic Serials and Newspapers in the Libraries of the Republic of Azerbaijan* (with T. Atabaki), (London, 1995); *Comintern Eastern Policy and Iran (1919-1943)* (Baku, 2001); *Union Catalogue of Persian, Arabic, Ottoman Turkish, Kurdish an Azerbaijan Serials and Newspapers in the Libraries of the Republic of Azerbaijan and the Republic of Georgia* with Touraj Atabaki, Grigol Beradze and George Sanikidze (Tehran, 2006). The range of her scientific interests, geography and topics of scientific publications are as follows: political history of Caucasus, Azerbaijan, Iran and Turkey in the first half of the twentieth century, history of the press of these countries, history of ideologies, history of Islam, history of Comintern, history of national-liberation movements, theoretical aspects and history of repressions and deportations, and historiography of every day life of Iranian migrants in Soviet Caucasus.

Index